THE
FIRST
GLOBAL
REVOLUTION

THE
FIRST
GLOBAL
REVOLUTION

A Report by the Council of The Club of Rome

ALEXANDER KING
& BERTRAND SCHNEIDER

Pantheon Books   *New York*

Library of Congress Cataloging-in-Publication Data
King, Alexander.
    The first global revolution : a report by the Council of The
Club of Rome / by Alexander King and Bertrand Schneider.
        p.   cm.
    Includes bibliographical references.
    1. Economic forecasting.   2. Economic history—1971-
    3. World politics—1985–1995.   I. Schneider, Bertrand.
II. Club of Rome. Council.   III. Title.
HC59.K479   1991   330′.01′12—dc20   91-20410
    ISBN 0-679-73825-8

Book Design by Fearn Cutler

Manufactured in the United States of America

3 5 7 9 8 6 4 2

"Ah love! Could thou and I with fate conspire, to grasp this sorry scheme of things entire, would not we shatter it to bits and then, remould it nearer to the heart's desire."

Omar Khayyam

CONTENTS

Foreword

THE YEAR 1968 WAS THE YEAR OF THE Great Divide. It marked the end as well as the zenith of the long postwar period of rapid economic growth in the industrialized countries. But it was also a year of social unrest with the eruption of student uprisings in many countries and other manifestations of alienation and countercultural protest. In addition it was at that time that general and vocal public awareness of the problems of the environment began to emerge.

A number of individuals close to decision-making points became concerned about the apparent incapability of governments and the international organisations of foreseeing, or even attempting to foresee, the consequences of substantial material growth without sufficient thought as to the quality aspects of the life that unprecedented general affluence should make possible. It was felt that the creation of a group of independent thinkers concerned with the longer term and deeper issues would be useful in complementing the work of the formal organisations.

The Club of Rome arose that year from these considerations. At present, it comprises one hundred independent individuals from fifty-three countries. It has absolutely no political ambition. Its members represent a wide diversity of cultures, ideologies, professions and disciplines, and are united in a common concern for the future of humanity. It chose as its initial theme, "The Predicament of Mankind."

From the outset, the Club's thinking has been governed by three related conceptual patterns:

- adopting a global approach to the vast and complex problems of a world in which interdependence among the nations within a single planetary system is constantly growing;

- focusing on issues, policies and options in a longer-term perspective than is possible for governments, which respond to the immediate concerns of an insufficiently informed constituency;

- seeking a deeper understanding of the interactions within the tangle of contemporary problems—political, economic, social, cultural, psychological, technological and environmental—for which the Club of Rome adopted the term "the world problematique."

The world problematique has become, as it were, the trademark of the Club. We define it as the massive and untidy mix of intertwining and interrelated difficulties and problems that form the predicament in which humanity finds itself. For our present purposes we have coined a corresponding term, "the world resolutique," to connote a coherent, comprehensive and simultaneous attack to resolve as many as possible of the diverse elements of the problematique, or at least to point out tracks to solutions and more effective strategies. By the resolutique, we do not suggest a grand attack on the totality of the problematique in all its diversity. This would be impossible. Our proposal is rather a simultaneous attack on its main elements with, in every case, careful consideration of reciprocal impact from each of the others. It seems that in a world that is increasingly immobilized by bureaucracies, there is a growing role for flexible and informal groups such as the Club of Rome to take initiatives.

Our first publication, *The Limits to Growth*, appeared in 1972 as a report to (rather than by) the Club of Rome. The study, commissioned by the Club, was accomplished by an international team of professors and researchers at MIT using the system dynamics methodology of Jay Forrester. This was a pioneering attempt to project in interaction a number of quantifiable elements of the problematique. The report and the controversy it generated immediately gave the Club of Rome worldwide visibility or, as some would say, notoriety. The report has sold some 10 million copies in over thirty languages and has had a considerable political impact.

The Limits to Growth achieved its main objective: the stimulation of a great debate on growth and society throughout the world and an increased awareness of the interactions that take place among the elements of the problematique. The Club was widely criticized for what was seen as advocacy of a zero growth economy. This was never our conviction. We fully accepted the pressing need for material growth in the poor countries of the world, but warned of the consequences of an unthinking pursuit of indiscriminate growth by the industrialized countries, depletion of the world resource base, deterioration of the environment and the domination of material values in society.

Since 1972 the Club has published eighteen reports on a wide variety of issues. The second of these, *Mankind at the Turning Point*, by Professors Eduard Pestel and Mihajlo Mesarovic, was also a computerised growth model, but it took regional situations into account. It included a strong warning of the high costs in terms of money and human suffering which would result from delay in taking action.

Two decades later the contemporary problematique remains the same in its underlying causes as that of 1972, but it differs in its mix of issues and its points of emphasis. Humanity will always have to live with the problematique of its time, no matter how effective the resolutique has been in the past. Changing situations, and notably those arising from the solution of past problems, give rise to new difficulties which, as always, interact. Furthermore, in times of rapid change, such as the present, the mix of problems and the understanding of their relative importance is likely to change rapidly. This is partly because some of our perceptions have become clearer and partly because new knowledge has identified new dangers. Of course, the two most dominant elements are probably those of the population explosion in the South and of the only recently recognized macroeffects of man on his environment, which were exactly the two central preoccupations in *The Limits to Growth*. But new factors, such as changes in human behaviour, the emergence of seemingly irrational movements, including terrorism, and the growth of individual and collective overt selfishness thrown up by our materialistic society, have definitely become elements of today's problematique. Such matters are obviously relevant in considering the present situation.

The human being both creates the problematique and suffers its consequences. The problematique therefore demands a systematic analysis that pays due attention not only to what is regarded as rational behaviour, but also to instinctive and apparently irrational elements inherent in human nature that make for an uncertain world.

If the Club is to live up to its role, it is essential that we reexamine the problematique, attempt to elucidate some of its interactions and issue warnings as to the consequences and trends determined by the persistence of present economic systems and human behaviour. With the possible exception of the nuclear threat, the dangers to humanity are probably greater and more imminent than were those in 1972 and we shall, no doubt, be accused as before of being harbingers of doom and gloom. This may well be our role and our glory. Doomsaying is, however, by no means our sole or even central role and intention. It is but a necessary prelude to "doombreaking." *The Limits to Growth* was never intended as a prophecy, but rather as a warning of what might happen if policies were not changed in order to prove its extrapolations wrong. A preventive approach such as this carries with it the responsibility of putting forward suggested remedies.

Ricardo Díez-Hochleitner,
President of The Club of Rome

"No generation has ever liked its prophets, least of all those who point out the consequences of bad judgment and lack of foresight.

The Club of Rome can take pride in the fact that it has been unpopular for the last twenty years. I hope it will continue for many years to come to spell out the unpalatable facts and to unsettle the conscience of the smug and the apathetic."

> Prince Philip, Duke of Edinburgh
> Message to the Twentieth Anniversary
> Conference of The Club of Rome
> Paris 1988

Acknowledgments

We would like to express our special gratitude and thanks to Club of Rome members Martin Lees *and* Donald Michael, *whose work with the Council has been a precious and indispensable contribution to the ideas and thoughts presented herein.*

We would equally like to thank Patrice Blank, Richard Carey *and* Alexander Peckham *for their sharp appraisal and enlightened counsel,* Soyo Graham-Stuart, Nicole Rosensohn *and* Marina Urquidi *for their criticism, advice, suggestions and strong support, as well as* Fabienne Bouton *for her unending patience during the composition of this book.*

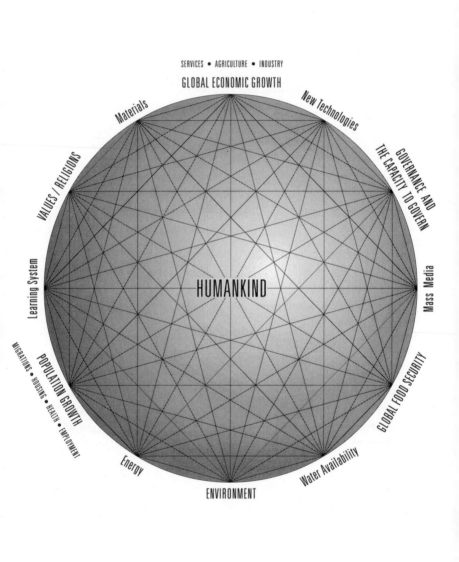

SERVICES • AGRICULTURE • INDUSTRY

GLOBAL ECONOMIC GROWTH

New Technologies

Materials

GOVERNANCE AND
THE CAPACITY TO GOVERN

VALUES / RELIGIONS

Learning System

Mass Media

HUMANKIND

POPULATION GROWTH

MIGRATIONS • HOUSING • HEALTH • EMPLOYMENT

GLOBAL FOOD SECURITY

Energy

Water Availability

ENVIRONMENT

Introduction

HUMANKIND SEEMS TO BE GRIPPED BY A FIN-de-siècle attitude of uncertainty at the threshold of the new century, but the end of a millennium brings a still deeper mystique with its widespread weight of rapid change and the uncertainty it carries with it.

The topic of recent Club of Rome meetings has been "The Great Transition." We are convinced that we are in the early stages of the formation of a new type of world society which will be as different from today's as was that of the world ushered in by the Industrial Revolution from the society of the long agrarian period that preceded it. The initial, but by no means only motor force of this change has been the emergence of a cluster of advanced technologies, especially those made possible by microelectronics and the new discoveries of molecular biology. These are creating what is variously called the information society, the postindustrial society or the service society, in which employment, life-style and prospects, material and otherwise, will be very different from those of today for every inhabitant.

We need only mention the population explosion in the Southern countries, the probability of deep change and disturbance of world climate, the precarious nature of global food security, doubts about energy availability and the vast changes taking place in the geopolitical situation, all of which interact within the complex of the problematique. We are convinced that the magnitude of these changes amounts to a major revolution on a worldwide scale.

The years 1989 and 1990 were years when history speeded up its course: communist regimes in Eastern Europe collapsed, East and West Germany became a single nation again, the 1990 invasion of Kuwait by Iraq provoked a deadly crisis in the Persian Gulf. And though these were by no means the only events of the period, they were by far the most spectacular. Despite their geographic dispersal, they were interconnected: the end of the cold war and of the East–West tension blew the lid off the world pressure cooker and enabled latent conflicts to blow up in the open and long-repressed aspirations to express themselves forcefully.

In the coming years, it is very likely that other events will have come to the forefront in the world while today's will have been pushed into the background. The Gulf War is the first illustration of a series of phenomena that will most certainly lie heavy on the world in the coming decades. It is in many ways a warning signal and should lead to a new vision of international relations.

The ending of the cold war has led to the awakening of numerous expressions of nationalism that had been stifled under the lid of East–West tension and will inevitably produce conflicts of varying degrees.

It confirms the tension which will continue to grow between the rich countries and the poor countries, between the North and the South, while the injustice and humiliation it breeds is found especially and increasingly unbearable by the Arab–Muslim countries.

The war has also been a demonstration of a new attempt by the United States to reassert its hegemonic presence in a number of regions of the world while putting its force at the service of right and legalism. The ambiguity of American policy, despite the fact that it has often shown proof of goodwill, is not going to make the international relations of the United States any easier in the future.

Finally, we have to stress that the process of disarmament that was undertaken between the United States and the Soviet Union is a positive—but not sufficient—element. Disarmament in high-risk zones and a strict control by the United Nations of high-tech arms sales have to be priorities if we expect to prevent other confrontations, as bloody and paradoxical as those that were induced by the war in the Gulf.

Will the budding democracy in Benin, as that in the Eastern European and Latin American countries, grow strong and spread, or will their failure to do so lead back to authoritarian governments? Will regimes that seem today to be firmly established be able to stand up to the pressure of populations, most of which are under twenty years of age and demanding a roof, a job and a means to survive and to live? No one knows.

There is, however, an indisputable fact: the world economic discrepancies, the flagrant inequalities, the vast and extreme poverty vis-à-vis an excess of wealth carry all sorts of tensions and conflicts showing up here and there in the most diverse geographic zones. They are signs that mark this first global revolution and illustrate the uncertainty with which the future of the planet is struck.

But why do we regard the contemporary threats and changes as the first global revolution? The change from the hunting and gathering phase to one of settled farming that probably originated in the discovery by some intelligent women of the possibility of domesticating food plants may have taken some tens of thousands of years to spread throughout the world. The Industrial Revolution that began in the United Kingdom some two centuries ago is as yet geographically incomplete. The present brutal changes are taking place everywhere simultaneously from causes which are likewise ubiquitous, thus causing the *Sturm und Drang* of a universal revolution. The worldwide significance of this revolution becomes vastly greater if one considers that its mismanagement could endanger the whole human race.

The new society is emerging from the chrysalis of the old societies, often archaic and decadent; its evolution is complex and uncertain and its manifestations are difficult to decipher, making the tasks of the decision makers of both public and private sectors more difficult than ever and inducing a permanent questioning on the part of all thinking individuals. Elements or transitional facets of the new society are appearing here and there without obvious ties between them.

The global revolution has no ideological basis. It is being shaped by an unprecedented mixture of geo-strategic earthquakes and of social, economic, technological, cultural and ethical factors. Combinations of these factors lead to unpredictable situations. In this transitional period, humanity is therefore facing a double challenge: having to grope its way towards an understanding of the new world with so many as yet hidden facets and also, in the mists of uncertainty, to learn how to manage the new world and not be managed by it. Our aim must be essentially normative: to visualize the sort of world we would like to live in, to evaluate the resources—material, human and moral— to make our vision realistic and sustainable and then to mobilize the human energy and political will to forge the new global society.

In matters of public concern, as in other areas of human interest, fashions prevail. Yesterday the nuclear problem was uppermost; later the population explosion reached the headlines; today the environment is à-la-mode and concern with population has receded. The energy prospects are as yet seldom mentioned publicly, but the events in the Middle East are already making this the new fashion. The need is to consider all these together as essential angles of illumination in the kaleidoscope of planetary change.

In this tangle of change it is important as never before to look beyond the pressing issues of the moment to the forces beyond the horizon. Forecasting is both necessary and will necessarily be a relative failure. Simple extrapolation of existing trends will not give us realistic answers. *The Limits to Growth*[1] had

[1] This was the first Report to the Club of Rome (Meadows, 1972).

developed an interactive simulation model that produced a variety of scenarios which had considerable significance regarding what was to be prevented. In some fields such as technology and industry long-term forecasting is indispensable and efforts in that direction are being made by some of the most forward-looking corporations, which are struggling to invent new methodologies for planning in uncertainty.

In the thirties, the American president Franklin D. Roosevelt commissioned his administration to undertake a vast study of the coming technologies. When the study was published it made a very big impression. Indeed, it was enthralling. There was just one problem: it had not predicted the coming of television, nor that of plastic, or jet planes, or organ transplants, or laser beams, not even of ball-point pens![2]

One aspect of the contemporary situation is an increasing awareness that the human race, in pursuit of material gain by exploitation of nature, is racing towards destruction of the planet and itself. The threat of nuclear destruction, although less imminent, is always with us and the possibility of irreversible climatic change with only dimly foreseeable consequences is an imminent menace. Such ingredients of the present problematique are global in character and cannot be tackled by even the largest powers in isolation. Only if all inhabitants of the planet realize that

[2]See Giesbert, 1990.

they are facing immediate and common dangers can a universal political will be generated for common action to achieve humanity's survival. This is why we call for the creation of world solidarity. The term *solidarity* has been greatly misused and seriously devalued. Its application to circumstances in which motivations for common belief or action were too weak have given it a somewhat utopian and insubstantial connotation. In present circumstances, however, the level of common danger to the future well-being of all the inhabitants of the planet gives it such enhanced force that it plainly has to be regenerated.

We have voluntarily presented a simplified version of things: many of the phenomena mentioned here would have to be analysed both much more deeply and more subtly. This would require numerous and weighty volumes.

Our option was different. Our wish was briefly—even if superficially and incompletely—to lay out elements that may already be known in order to show how they interact, and through their entanglement to state our outlook on the world problematique today as clearly as possible.

We do not presume to draw up a blueprint of concrete actions for the salvation of the world. Nevertheless, our analysis of the situation encourages us to make a number of practical proposals, to suggest lines of possible action and to indicate necessary changes in attitude.

Never before has humanity possessed as it does today the knowledge and the skills, the resources and the cohesion to shape a better world. This should generate a resounding hope for all people. Yet there is a widespread sense of unease and fear of impending changes which, in impinging on the still undigested changes of recent decades, will add to the uncertainty. This very uncertainty, together with the broken rigidities of the past and the new hopes for the future, is an enormous opportunity for reshaping the world society. The tragedy of the human condition is that we have not yet reached a position to realize our potential. We see the world and its resources being grossly mismanaged, yet we are lulled by the complacency of our leaders and our own inertia and resistance to change. Time is running out. Some problems have already reached a magnitude which is beyond the point of successful attack and the costs of delay are monstrously high. Unless we wake up and act quickly it could be too late.

This book is organised in two parts. The first deals with the problematique and purports to present the main changes of the last two decades, to describe the malaise which they have caused and to outline some of the most important issues and dangers which humanity has to face in unity. The second part approaches the resolutique and attempts to present a number of actions which, at this stage, seem especially necessary to pursue. Finally we return to the need to generate world solidarity.

The First Global Revolution is written for all those who have the spark of the explorer, the discoverer, the risk-taker—the learner. For those who go through the swamp or up the mountain because they're made that way. These are the people we shall have to count on to face the appalling issues described herein, to set the goals and try to reach them and to learn from their failures and successes, to go on trying—learning.

Finally, it is addressed to those who are concerned with the future of the planet and of humankind, and hopes to sharpen their concern. Also it may help to awaken concern in others. Above all, it is addressed to the young, so they may assess more coherently the state of a world they have inherited from earlier generations and may be inspired to work for the construction of a new and sustainable society, capable of providing a life of quality and modest prosperity for their children and generations to come.

This is the spirit in which we offer these ideas and proposals for action, for learning our way into the future.

I

THE
PROBLEMATIQUE

I

A WHIRLWIND
OF CHANGE

JANUARY 1969: TWENTY-ONE-YEAR-OLD JAN Pallach sets fire to himself on Wenceslas Square in Prague to protest the occupation of Czechoslovakia by Soviet tanks.

December 1989: Dissident writer Vaclav Havel is elected President of the Republic of Czechoslovakia.

September 1973: Democracy in the Republic of Chili is swept away by a bloody military coup (10,000 dead in six months, 90,000 arrested, and 163,000 forced into exile).

December 1989: First democratic elections since September 1970 puts an end to the military regime in Chili.

The seeds of the coming global revolution have been germinating slowly over many years, during which conditions of complexity, uncertainty and rapid change have appeared as never before and are beginning to overwhelm the capacity of the world governance system. Indeed, governments never like

3

change; wedded to the status quo, they react to symptoms but seldom to causes which tend to be regarded with suspicion as possibly leading to "subversive" changes. One of the most obvious aspects of human frailty is too great a concentration on the immediate, with too little care for future consequences—an insistence on immediate gratification. This applies to institutions as well as to people. Governments operating under the tyranny of the next election focus on the present issues and avoid the more distant but frequently more fundamental matters. Corporations likewise bow to the tyranny of next year's bottom line, even if both governments and enterprises look beyond the next election or annual report in much of what they do.

The Club of Rome was founded in the year 1968 when the economic growth mania was at its height.

Soon after the publication of its first report, *The Limits to Growth*[1] in 1972, the world was hit by the oil crisis. This had many repercussions on the economy and society; it had a strong impact on the world investment pattern and caused many policy modifications, for example, in the attitude of the United States to the Middle East. The crisis was a clear warning to the industrialized countries regarding the vulnerability of their economies to the security of supply of raw materials and energy, dependent on events in distant places largely beyond their control.

The oil crisis also brought home to most of the oil-importing developing countries the extent of their reliance upon cheap fuels, with hardly any local energy alternative; it also led these countries into excessive

[1]Meadows, 1972.

external indebtedness designed not so much to foster development as merely to pay the oil bill.

The oil crisis and other factors have led to a considerable lowering of economic growth rates from the high levels of the previous decades. Achievements of economic growth, however, still remain the main explicit goal of economic policy, with too little consideration of differential needs and quality aspects. How far the published growth figures reflect real increases in human welfare, however, is open to question. Much of what is counted as growth is probably not growth at all. For example, in the United States of President Reagan, growth figures concealed overconsumption and public underinvestment, deterioration of the infrastructure, decay of the inner cities and social deterioration. Nor is there any evidence that growth in the North leads in time to development in the South.

> "In today's world all curves are exponential. It is only in mathematics that exponential curves grow to infinity. In real life they either break down catastrophically or they saturate gently. It is our duty as thinking people to strive towards a gentle saturation although this poses new and very difficult questions."
>
> Dennis Gabor

> "If, for example, an economy grows at an annual rate of 5%, it would, by the end of the next century, reach a level of 500 times greater (or 50,000% higher) than the current level."
>
> Eduard Pestel*

In 1968 few could have foreseen the fundamental political changes we have recently witnessed. Already the political dominance of the two superpowers was beginning to dwindle, but the cold war ruled not only East–West relations but defined the whole international system, torn apart by ideological polarisation. The recent events in the Soviet Union and Eastern Europe have therefore shaken not only the region but the whole planet. The collapse of economic communism and the disintegration of the Warsaw Pact bloc of nations has aroused great hopes and is invested with great dangers. The situation is extremely fluid, has few constraints and its consolidation offers great opportunities for the structuring and renewal of a much wider region, and possibly of the world system as a whole.

History is unlikely to provide another opportunity as open and promising as today's, so it is essential for humanity to find the wisdom to exploit it. This unfreezing of the geopolitical rigidities of the last forty-five years is one, but only one, of the elements shaping the global revolution. Entangled with many

* Former minister of Culture, Science and Technology of Lower Saxony, former member of the Executive Committee of The Club of Rome (Pestel, 1989).

other forces of change it has made the future shape of the world still more uncertain.

Throughout the period since 1968 the world has lived under the shadow of the nuclear bomb, but now, with East and West willing to put an end to the cold war, a new climate is dawning in international affairs despite the setbacks recorded in the beginning of 1991. Although nuclear annihilation no longer seems imminent, the threat has certainly not been banished; indeed it may exist as long as the planet is peopled by humans. Great vigilance is essential, not only with regard to the intentions and behaviour of the present nuclear powers but also in order to curtail nuclear proliferation and to ensure that smaller nations now developing nuclear devices are persuaded or prevented from using them in local wars against neighbouring states. This requires a new strategy on a global scale, quite different from the bipolar approach of the cold war period. Humanity will have to be forever on guard against the arising of insane leaders of charisma, capable of hypnotising whole nations and willing to destroy the world rather than to go down in defeat. Such was the case in January 1991 with the Gulf War. Who can foretell the medium- to long-term consequences of the war on the environment as well as on the geopolitical balance of the Middle East?

Despite present difficulties and contradictions, hope still exists for the continued progress in disarmament negotiations in terms of conventional arms and of chemical and biological weapons. Wars on the world scale must be avoided; the power and sophistication of modern weapons make winning out of the question and the high cost of their development and manufacture a permanent burden, inhibiting economic and social development. Local wars are likely to continue until some overall global harmony is established. In the period under review some fifty such wars have raged and there has been a considerable build-up of arms in the less developed countries, much to the detriment of their development possibilities.

The economies of the industrialized nations benefit greatly from the sale of arms. The business is highly competitive and contributes substantially to the encouragement of war. Furthermore, it can easily boomerang and hit the nations supplying the arms, as has been the case in the Falklands and Gulf wars. The latter in particular has highlighted the need, in the interest of humanity as a whole, to control the arms industry, both that operated by the governments themselves and that operated by private contractors.

It must be emphasized here that peace is not merely the absence of war and that even without war, conflicts will continue and will change in character; examples are trade wars, totalitarian regimes and economic colonialism. Inequitable distribution of resources is certainly one of the strongest and most insidious triggers of conflict.

The extensive disarmament—achieved or planned —should set free resources, human and material, that can be used for more positive purposes such as restructuring of the economies of Eastern Europe, providing more investment in Africa and Latin America and making possible environmental renewal. The process of disarmament, however, brings its own problems. For some countries, and particularly the Soviet Union, the process is difficult on account of the need to rehouse large numbers of discharged soldiers and to absorb them in a precarious and changing economy. As for redistribution, the sums saved can all too easily become unidentifiable within the finances of national treasures or indirectly come under the control of narrow vested interests.

ECONOMIC CHANGE

Great changes have also taken place on the economic front and will be analysed in more detail in Chapter 3. After the period of rapid growth, recession set in simultaneously with the oil crisis and the recycling of the Arab surplus. During the last two decades the economic centre of gravity has moved towards the Pacific region, with the amazing success of the Japanese industrial economy. Japan now accounts for some 38% of the world's total financial capacity; however, this is now falling rapidly with the decline in the Tokyo stock market and falling real estate prices. Japan has not yet learned how to exercise its strength even if it has contributed to assist the debtors in alleviating their burden under the Brady plan. Its political moves are cautious and tentative and, as yet, it is not internationally as effective as it should be.

One of the outstanding facts of recent years has been the progressive conversion to a market economy, which seems to be turning into the common denominator of most countries of the world. Open competition, sometimes brutal, on both the international and national scales has convinced political leaders, as well as consumers, voters and the community at large of every shade that the vitality of it is irreplaceable. Private business is considered to be its motor, profit to be necessary for investment and the financial market to be the inevitable meeting point between savings and investment.

The effectiveness of the market as a social institution for harnessing human productive energies and meeting human needs is now universally acknowledged. But market mechanisms alone cannot cope with global problems that require a long-term strategic approach or involve distributional issues. They cannot by themselves solve problems related to energy, environment, fundamental research or fairness —only public intervention, based on political processes and often using market mechanisms as an instrument of public policy, can deal with these problems.

Market forces can have dangerous side effects because they are not founded on general interest. International financial speculation is a particularly eloquent example of the excesses due to market forces gripped by the madness of profit under any circumstances. Speculation then becomes a game that is disconnected from economic realities: it escapes from the hands of men to be run by computer software and reach new dimensions and velocity thanks to the information society. Some efforts—still modest, for the task is tremendous—are leading a first attack on outrageous underground trafficking through its financial manifestations: the money-laundering for drug-traffic or unauthorized arms sales, for instance, is being uncovered by breaking the seal of secrecy on numbered bank accounts. It is hoped that such efforts will be enlarged and become the object of a true international co-operation.

Neither can we ignore geostrategic change. We are currently witnessing the emergence of three gigantic trading and industrial economic groupings. The North American market in which Canada has now joined the United States and which Mexico is expected to join, will inevitably continue to be an industrial and postindustrial group of great power. Its immediate future, however, is clouded by the immense deficit which, amazingly, the United States has allowed to accumulate in recent years.

The development of the European Community, despite the years of hesitation, is now acquiring substance as its members see tangible economic and political advantages in co-operation and devise new mechanisms for it. As 1993 approaches, with its completion of economic integration, the Community has begun discussion of political unity. This has become especially urgent with the reunification of East and West Germany. A Community embracing the whole of Western Europe and later joined by its Eastern neighbours—whose transformed economies should make this possible—would constitute a second bloc of great strength. Despite present confusion, it is not impossible that the European republics of the Soviet Union will eventually follow the same road, thus constructing Europe "from the Atlantic to the Ural Mountains," as was expressed by Charles de Gaulle in 1960.[2]

---

[2]In a television interview during his visit to Paris in 1989, Michael Gorbachev quoted this same statement by de Gaulle when referring to Europe.

The third bloc consists of Japan and the ASEAN[3] countries, including for example Thailand, Indonesia or Malaysia, which are growing rapidly. Later, perhaps Australia and New Zealand, which have strong trading links with the other Pacific countries, may find themselves in this grouping. Even at this early stage of development, the existence of these three blocs signifies an utterly different world pattern of trade and industry.

These new blocs are not restrictive, on the whole, to outside trading countries although they do have certain nontariff barriers and disguised protection. There is much trade among the groupings. What should in any event be emphasized is that there has been a very rapid change in technology and in the speed of its application, which has modified the relative strength of different trade groupings, especially of the Japan/ASEAN grouping.

This prospect is of great concern to other regions of the world. Latin America, close to the United States, but with a different ethos, is particularly perplexed. While initiatives from its neighbour in the North are on the horizon, it is also stretching out towards Europe, with Spain playing a special role through its membership in the European Economic Community and other European multilateral agencies and councils. The Soviet Union, in disarray, is not yet in a position to deal with this situation and China, after the brutal events of 1989, remains an enigma, while impoverished Africa hardly appears on the world economic map.

The South-Asian region, dominated by the huge

[3]Association of South-East Asian Nations.

geographical and demographic bulk of India, has made some progress, but it is still uncertain whether it will be able to make the sort of economic breakthrough that has occurred in South-East Asia. Population control here is the key.

Great care will have to be taken in forging the links between the evolving economic blocs on the one hand and the countries still outside. Some are already referring to the latter superciliously as the residual countries. As these include most of the poorer countries, the new economic pattern necessitates a fundamentally different approach to the problem of overall development including a conceptual switch from aid to partnership. The Gulf crisis may be a foretaste of many conflicts to come, not necessarily only in the form of North–South confrontation, but related to resources including energy and food availability, population pressures and ethnic and religious animosities. In a pluralistic world with many cultural, ethnic and religious differences, acceptance of others is essential and will have to be manifested in both word and deed. It has to be appreciated that consideration of the Western, rationalist view of world problems is difficult for many countries and may at times be wrong. Indeed the Iraqi position in 1991 represents a rejection of Western values, largely supported by Arab–Muslim public opinion.

Conflicts in a world dominated by huge trade blocs are likely to be very different from those of today's world of nation states. Wars between countries within a bloc or between blocs are more likely to be economic than military. In this connection, the future role of the transnational corporations will probably become increasingly important, since their interests and structures would permeate all the blocs.

THE INTERDEPENDENCE OF THE NATIONS

A further feature of the geopolitical scene is a belated recognition of the essentially global nature of many of the contemporary problems, which cannot be solved or even approached realistically by individual countries in isolation. This has long been the case in the economic field. One has only to remember how quickly the Wall Street crash in the 1930s spread to become a world depression, and how mass unemployment tends to appear simultaneously in many countries. This was no doubt the inevitable consequence of the great expansion of world trade which this century has witnessed. More recently global problems of a different nature have arisen. These range from environmental issues to "Law of the Sea" negotiations and international finance. Recognition of this new situation, awareness of which came very slowly, is illustrated by the mushrooming of intergovernmental conferences and those of specialized professional and scientific organisations during our period of review. It is doubtful if present international structures are sufficiently effective to deal with this new situation. The United Nations and its specialized agencies, which were founded in the postwar euphoria, were designed to meet the needs of a much simpler world situation and are increasingly inappropriate to today's needs. The present deidealized circumstances provide an opportunity as well as an imperative need for restructuring the United Nations system, reallocating the functions of the various agencies and programmes and providing a new focus. Current difficulties in revitalizing UNESCO show how difficult this will be. We should also underline the rising role and effectiveness of national and international NGOs[4] in various fields.

Concern with the global environment is giving rise to a number of ad hoc probings at different levels, including that of heads of government. As yet such attempts are avoiding the fundamental issues. It is to be hoped that common and universal action to combat such global problems will surmount interbloc rivalry.

This leads to consideration of the great increase in the interdependence of the nations which our period has seen. The growth of economic communities, the need for a common approach to the global issues, the immense expansion of international communications and the activities of the transnational corporations are some of the contributing factors. In addition, the spread of technology and its services throughout the world, the need for common standards, codes of agreed-upon practice, distribution of radio wavelengths and a thousand other technical agreements represent in their totality a spreading web of interdependence and a de facto erosion of national sovereignty not yet fully realized.

[4]Non-Governmental Organisations.

> "The cult of sovereignty has become mankind's major religion. Its God demands human sacrifice."
>
> Arnold Toynbee

The very concept of sovereignty proclaimed as sacrosanct by all governments is under challenge and not only as the result of the development of regional communities. Indeed, many smaller countries already have very little control over their own affairs in consequence of decisions taken outside their territories, such as the establishment of commodity prices or interest rates, or by economic policies modified to obtain IMF[5] funding. Erosion of sovereignty may be for most countries a positive move towards the new global system in which the nation-state will, in all probability, have a diminishing significance. In the case of most of the sub-Saharan countries of Africa, however, the maintenance and even the reinforcement of sovereignty is essential in present circumstances. These countries are intrinsically artificial, derived through the process of decolonialization from the arbitrary carve-up of the Continent by the former colonial powers.

Here it is necessary to distinguish between the Nation and the State. The African state may consist of a number of tribes which are, in reality, nations. A country such as Chad is politically a state but is not likely ever to become a nation. The situation is further complicated by the fact that important nation-tribes may be distributed between several states.

[5]International Monetary Fund.

Recognition of the sovereignty of such states may therefore be necessary to encourage coherence and common identity, but should lead to regional organisation. In Latin America the notion of sovereignty is still strongly defended as a juridical defence against the great powers.

A new concept has emerged as a consequence of artificially created states with nation-peoples dispersed among different states: "the right to intervene" was recently put into practice on a French initiative and soon after with United Nations blessings, by France, the United Kingdom and the United States. It consisted in a humanitarian operation within the state of Iraq in favour of the Kurdish people. Such a concept, if it were to be confirmed in the future, would represent a considerable evolution in international law, which for once would be more a reflection of humanitarian considerations than of constitutional rules and nationalist self-centeredness.

THE AWAKENING OF MINORITIES AND NATIONALISM

This brings us to an apparent paradox in world political trends. On the one hand, there is a tendency to create larger units, as in the case of the economic communities. Also the resolution of the global problems demand global action. On the other hand, there is a widespread public dislike of what is seen as excessive centralization. The dominance of large, faceless bureaucracies which appear to disregard the needs of individuals and of local communities is generally resented. The situation is particularly acute where such dominance impinges on the identity of ethnic minorities and we see in an ever increasing number of places how ethnic groups are becoming vocal and active in their demands for autonomy or independence. In Europe, for example, the Catalans and the Scots are asserting their nationhood, while the Irish, Basques and Corsicans have resorted to violence. Yugoslavia, which is an uneasy federation of republics with different historical traditions and ethnic mixes, threatens to disintegrate.

Without forgetting the ethnic diversity of China, most remarkable of all is the situation in the Soviet Union, the most ethnically heterogeneous of all federations, where the arrival of Glasnost and Perestroika has led to separatist movements among a dozen or more ethnically diverse republics. In America we are witnessing the collective awakening of American Indians who now have recourse to action. Hispanic and other unrepresented minorities have also increased their means of action.

These two apparently opposed trends are in reality compatible. The apparent conflict arises from the difficulty of reconciling them within the existing political system which is rigidly set on the model of the nation-state. What is needed is a reformulation of the appropriate levels of decision making to bring the points of decision as near as possible to those who enjoy or suffer their consequences. There appears to be a common human need for ethnic identity, deeply buried in the past of the human race. Equally, there appears to be a widespread tendency for people, even in ethnically homogeneous communities, to become identified with the affairs, prosperity and environment of their community. It is suggested that a greater number of points of decision making are necessary, ranging from the strictly local to the international. This could ease the load on central governments and help to humanize the system.

URBAN GROWTH

Urban growth has been a strong feature of the period and is set to continue. According to United Nations estimates, some 60% of the world population will be living in towns at the end of the century and there will be some thirty cities with more than 5 million inhabitants, with the largest, Mexico City, having 24–26 million. While this is a worldwide phenomenon, it is particularly marked in the developing countries where cities have mushroomed owing to a high birth rate in the cities themselves and an influx of peasants who have left the land to exchange urban for rural poverty. It is interesting to note that in the first city to reach 1 million inhabitants, London, more people died than were born up until 1840, with the increase coming essentially from rural emigration. In the developing countries today, this has reversed, with internal growth being the main factor of increase. This indicates how greatly sanitation and health have improved, despite the very difficult conditions of the urban poor.

Management of the mammoth cities such as Mexico, São Paulo, Lagos, Cairo or Calcutta is extremely difficult, especially since a large proportion of the urban dwellers are "unofficial," living in favellas or shantytowns with little or no sanitation, and are more or less outside the control of the authorities. Provision of water, health services, education, employment, urban transportation, control of pollution are some of the components of the complex of urban problems about which there is no experience on the present scale.

All over the developing regions, patterns of settlement and consequently life-style are changing rapidly, and quite large cities are springing up, often mainly as a sprawl of shantytowns completely lacking any adequate economic basis. In the Sahel region of Africa, for instance, towns such as Nouakchott, Bamako and Ouagadougou, until recently quiet administrative centres, have become vast urban slums with probably as many as 1 million inhabitants each, with all the explosive economic and psychological tensions from which they inevitably suffer. The new patterns of settlement and of excessively rapid urban expansion are partly the result also of high rates of population growth in the recent past.

DEVELOPMENT

Throughout the period under review, great efforts have been made to speed up the development of the poorer countries through massive programmes of aid, both bilateral and multilateral, capital and technical. A somewhat optimistic assessment of some aspects of these efforts was made by Mahbub Ul Haq: [6]

> Average life expectancy has increased by sixteen years, adult literacy by 40%, per capita nutritional levels by over 20%, and child mortality rates have been halved during this period. In fact, developing countries have achieved in the last thirty years the kind of real human progress that it took industrial

[6]Special Adviser to UNDP (United Nationes Development Programme) Administrator; personal communication, 1989.

countries nearly a century to accomplish. While the income gap between North and South is still very large—with the average income in the South being 6% of that in the North—the human gaps have been closing fast: average life expectancy in the South is by now 80% of the Northern average level, adult literacy 66% and nutritional level 85%. It is true that the past record of the developing world is uneven, as between various regions and countries and even within countries. It is also true that there is still a large unfinished agenda of human development—with one-fourth of the people in developing countries still deprived of basic human needs, a minimum income level and decent social services. But the overall policy conclusion is that the development process does work, that international development co-operation has made a significant difference and that the remaining agenda of human development should be manageable in the 1990s if development priorities are properly chosen.

Nevertheless, results have been uneven and often disappointing. Hunger, malnutrition, disease and poverty still afflict a large proportion of humanity and are aggravated by the population explosion, droughts and many local wars. The purchase of arms by many of the poorer countries from the industrialized nations not only represents a huge economic burden but encourages military adventure. The arms trade in effect produces a considerable flow of wealth from the poor to the rich. Also a number of leading developing countries have created an increasingly important arms industry, partly for export.

Scientific and technological advances in the industrialized countries tend to increase the economic disparities between the rich and the poor countries and to inhibit the latter from undertaking technological innovations. The poor countries, lacking industrial, technological and scientific structures and trained managerial capacity, have been unable to assimilate much of the technology and know-how available to them. Technology transfer was assumed to be the obvious method of introducing new processes and new industries into the less-developed countries, but it has often failed, sometimes as a result of selecting inappropriate processes or unsuitable industries and sometimes, with key-in-hand transfer, because of insufficient preparation and absence of management, maintenance and marketing skills in the receiving country. Often new technologies have been introduced for import substitutions which have not achieved a level of quality to insure international competitivity.

Too great a priority has been given to large-scale and sometimes dramatic schemes, for example, in the building of large dams to provide hydroelectric power and make possible extensive irrigation systems. Too often the dam reservoirs have silted up and the irrigation water become saline, while there has been little complementary industrial development and no rural electrification networks to consume the power. Also, in the design of such schemes too little attention has been given to social factors, including the displacement of large populations, fertile soil flooded in the reservoir collection areas and the spread of bilharziasis via the irrigation channels. In Africa, in particular, the fragmentation of the continent into too many small and not economically viable countries, each possessing too small markets, has limited the value of large-scale projects.

In agriculture, the Green Revolution, with the introduction of new and high-yielding varieties of wheat, maize and rice and intensive use of nitrogenous fertilizers has registered considerable success, especially in India and other Asiatic countries as well as Mexico, where the new farm technology started. This has enabled India to move rapidly from food deficit to a situation of marginal surplus. But here again there have been difficult social consequences. The system favours the medium and large-scale farmer and has led to displacement of peasant-farmers and rural migration to the cities. The energy-intensive nature of Green Revolution agriculture may also lead to difficulties when oil prices rise.

In other parts of the world and, once again especially in many African countries and in Latin America, insufficient attention has been given to agricultural development. Frequent droughts, increased populations of humans and animals, and local wars or internal conflicts have led to erosion of the resource base and marginalized large numbers of the rural poor. This has again thrown many people from the land and caused a rapid growth of the cities. It is in the urban areas that discontent and insurrection sprout so easily, and hence governments have yielded to the temptation of according priorities in their allocation of scarce resources to projects visibly of benefit to the city-dwellers. As a result of the low priority given to agriculture in many African and Latin America countries, these continents are likely to continue with a considerable food deficit for many years to come.

A further myth of development lore is that the benefits of economic development trickle down from the rich to the poor. This also is to be questioned. In India, for example, while the Green Revolution has provided food in plenty, there is little evidence of a commensurate diminution of hunger, malnutrition and poverty in rural areas.

It has been customary in recent decades to classify the countries of the world according to three economic categories—the First World of the industrialized market economy countries, the Second World of the state economy Marxist world, and the Third World of the less developed countries. With the virtual collapse of the state-directed economies, this classification now makes little sense and needs to be finally cast away, while the concept of the Third World has already become almost meaningless because of the wide diversity of economic conditions[7] and potentialities that the term embraces. To bunch together Saudi Arabia and Singapore, or Brazil, Botswana and Bangladesh is evidently absurd in that generalized statements of Third World problems have little or no relevance to individual cases. It is now more popular to refer to the developed countries as the North and the underdeveloped as the South. Despite the geographical anomaly of including Aus-

[7] A similar situation is arising concerning the so-called NICS (Newly Industrialized Countries). The term *NICS* has been used essentially to describe the spectacular developments in Hong Kong, Singapore, South Korea and Taiwan. Now other countries such as Indonesia, Malaysia, Thailand are also following the same path. Larger developing countries including Brazil, India and Mexico with an industrial base created years ago are also progressing rapidly in the use of new technologies but are in quite different categories. Thus we have a spectrum of different stages of industrialization.

tralia in the North, this nomenclature makes more sense, but the North–South separation detracts from a new need to regard the problems of development in a regional as well as in the global context of the rapidly changing world economic system.

Recent years have seen the accumulation of indebtedness in a number of countries. In the cases of Argentina, Brazil and Mexico this has reached stranglehold level and, while many lending agencies have considerably written off their bad debts and elsewhere some rescheduling has taken place, the debt situation remains grave, both for the development possibilities of the debtor countries and for the stability of the world financial system. In Africa, while indebtedness is much lower in absolute terms than that in Latin America, the debt-servicing burden is crippling. At a time when capital flow has turned to the needs of the Eastern European countries, less developed debtor countries see little hope of an alleviation of their situation. Most extraordinary of all is the fact that the United States has allowed itself to acquire an internal debt of U.S. $3.2 trillion (1989), greater that of any country in the world. This remains a dark stormcloud on the economic horizon.

The grave problems of world poverty, aggravated by population growth, could well give rise to great and disruptive disharmony on a world scale, the consequences of which the industrial countries could not escape. It is strongly in the self-interest of the rich countries that a new, powerful and radically different approach be taken to the problems of world development. With the metamorphosis of Eastern Europe, with its great need for capital, managerial and technological inflows, there is a real fear that the needs of the poor countries will be forgotten or relegated to a still-lower priority than the present one. This would be dangerous, not only for the poor countries but for the world as a whole.

THE POPULATION EXPLOSION

The problems of most developing countries are greatly exacerbated by the population explosion. World population, now just over 5 billion (from 1.8 billion in 1900), is expected to reach 6.2 billion in the year 2000 and more than 8.5 billion in 2025, according to median UN projections. India, for example, would grow from 819 million now to 1.446 billion, Nigeria from 105 to 301 million, and Mexico from 85 to 150 million. By far the greater part of population growth will take place in the less-developed regions of the world. Indeed, in the industrialized regions, demographic growth is very slow and in some cases even negative, posing to these countries a whole series of difficulties associated with aging populations.

At present the world's aggregate population is rising by 1 million persons every four to five days (reference here is to net growth, that is, births minus deaths). Although fertility rates are beginning to fall in some regions, because of the very low median age in some of the developing countries owing to recent explosion, the daily increase in absolute terms will be greater in 2000 than it is today. In these circumstances it is difficult to see how the necessary food, housing, health and educational facilities can be provided. Population growth is outstripping food production. In the years preceding the recent droughts, grain production of sub-Saharan Africa was increasing by about 1.6% per annum, with population growing by 3.1%, while in some countries where food shortages are the worst per capita production has fallen by about 2% per annum over the last decade. Furthermore, population growth is providing a greatly increased work force, mainly in places where there is already acute unemployment and poverty and extensive underemployment. The task of creating the millions of new jobs is indeed one of the most formidable tasks arising from the population explosion.

ENVIRONMENT

December 3, 1989. Bhopal, India: a leak at the Union Carbide pesticide factory poisons the air with methylisocyanide, killing 3,600 people and wounding 100,000, of which 50,000 remain permanently disabled.

April 26, 1986. Chernobyl, U.S.S.R.: an accident at the nuclear power station at Chernobyl destroys the reactor and projects five tons of fuel into the atmosphere (50 million curies of radiation). A radioactive cloud goes around the world, especially affecting Ukrania and Bielorussia (U.S.S.R.), Finland, Scandinavia, Poland, Germany, France. Immediate human consequences: thirty-two officially dead (twenty-nine from radiation), 150,000 people evacuated, 119 villages permanently abandoned, 499 seriously wounded, 600,000 exposed to radiation of which twelve have become invalid and 7,000 to 25,000 are expected to develop cancer. Food crops and animals exposed for several years to radiation all over Europe. In 1990, approximately 3 million persons under medical supervision, with reports of two persons dying daily as a consequence of the nuclear accident.

March 24, 1989. Prince William Bay, Alaska: American oil cargo ship SS Exxon Valdez runs aground, spilling 40,000 tons of oil and polluting over 1,744 kilometres of coast, killing 980 otters and 33,126 birds. U.S. $1.9 billion spent to clean up and in compensation to fishing villages.

A striking phenomenon of the period under review is widespread alarm at the deterioration of the environment, both rural and urban. Pollution phenomena arose as a consequence of the Industrial Revolution and are well documented in nineteenth-century literature, with Blake's "dark Satanic mills" of industrial England, the pea-soup fogs and the dirty rivers. A degree of control was gradually established in most countries through legislation, although heavy pollution of this sort persists in Eastern Europe as a heritage of the Marxist economy.

By 1968, however, a new level of concern had appeared. Industry had become much more sophisticated. Its output had diversified enormously, with products, intermediates and wastes, in many cases toxic and nonbiodegradable, diffusing into the biosphere. In addition, population increase and its concentration in huge cities, as well as the massive consumption of goods and materials, was making it ever more difficult to dispose of sewage and solid wastes. It had been assumed until recently that a benevolent Nature would forever absorb and neutralize the waste products of society in the air, the soil, the rivers and the oceans. This assumption no longer holds; we appear to have crossed a critical threshold, beyond which human impact on the environment threatens to be destructive and possibly irreversible.

Public concern was aroused by the publication of popular books such as Rachel Carson's *Silent Spring*[8] and E. F. Schumacher's *Small Is Beautiful.*[9]

By 1968 reactions became general and vocal with environmental and conservationist movements appearing everywhere.[10] In the industrialized countries as public pressures grew, governments took action. Environmental policies and environmental ministers sprouted and, since pollution is no respecter of political boundaries, the environmental issues reached the international conferences. Much improvement has resulted; many of the grosser manifestations of pollution have been eliminated as a result of legislative action. Adoption of principles such as "the polluter pays" have alerted industry to accept a new social responsibility; rivers have been cleaned up and air pollution reduced, and everywhere local groups are vigilant with regard to developments that might threaten the environment—sometimes with useful foresight and common sense and at other times with fanaticism.

An interesting development has been the way in which concerned public groups have consolidated to take direct political action. The arising of the green parties has been useful in forcing the traditional parties to take the environmental issues seriously, although it is difficult to foresee a lasting role for them or, for that matter, for any single-issue party. The

[8]Carson, 1963.
[9]Schumacher, 1973.
[10]The United Nations Conference on the Human Environment in Stockholm in 1977 was a landmark event.

"green movement," useful as it is, may inadvertently be diverting public attention from the longer-term and more serious environmental issues that we shall discuss later insofar as they impress the man in the street with the easily appreciated, immediately visible but strictly local damage.

> "Annihilating all that's made to a green thought in a green shade."
>
> Andrew Marvell,
> Seventeenth-century Caroline poet

Until recently most forms of environmental deterioration have been essentially local and could be eliminated by local and national action—at a cost, certainly, but one that could be borne. However, now environmental threats of a new order of magnitude and difficulty have been identified, which demand quite a different approach. These reside in a number of macropollution phenomena, global in scope and beyond the capacity of individual countries to eliminate. At present, there are four preoccupying cases of macropollution.

- Diffusion of toxic substances in the environment. These consist both of nonbiodegradable chemicals and also radioactive wastes. Initial concern was caused by the discovery of the widespread diffusion of DDT, which was detected even in penguin eggs in Antarctica. This suggested that the molecule might find its way into the human food chain and accumulate to a threshold of danger. Subsequently, many other toxic materials which diffuse widely have been identified, and it is suggested that virulently toxic materials threaten to penetrate into the main aquifers of the world within a few decades. Accumulation of toxic wastes, difficult to dispose of locally, have induced a number of industrialized countries to export their "cargoes of poison" to poor countries in Africa, willing to sell discharge rights. This is an immoral trade and its extension is to the detriment of the situation of the receiving country but also globally. As yet, there is no satisfactory solution to the disposal of radioactive wastes, which demand extremely long containment because of the very long half-life of many radioisotopes.

- Acidification of lakes and the destruction of forests as a result of attack by effluents, airborne from the chimneys of coal-burning power stations, steel mills, etc. This has been recognized for sometime now and has resulted in international complaints. For example, the lakes and forests of Eastern Canada suffer from the smoke of Pittsburgh and those of Scandinavia from the acid gases of the English Midlands and the Ruhr. Much can be done here on a local basis (for international as well as local results) by scrubbing flue gases, using odd low-sulphur oils and coals and other means, but it is a costly and difficult business. The mechanism of acidification is not fully understood; in addition to distant contamination, other agencies may be at work.

- Macropollution in the upper atmosphere caused by CFCs (chlorofluorohydrocarbons). These substances are chosen for their extreme stability under normal terrestial conditions and used as aerosol propellants and in refrigerators. Unfortunately, when they ascend to the upper atmosphere they decompose under the influence of high-intensity ultraviolet radiation and release chlorine, which attacks the stratospheric ozone. The discovery, a few years ago, of large holes in the ozone layer above Antarctica caused alarm that this layer was becoming depleted and might cause increased ultraviolet radiation at the earth's surface, which would greatly increase the risk of skin cancer and other diseases. The CFCs were soon detected as the culprits. International action was obviously necessary if this was to be avoided; subsequent efforts to achieve this are highly suggestive of the type of international negotiation that will be necessary in other and more complicated cases. Intrinsically the situation here is rather simple, since the number of chemical plants producing CFCs in the world is quite small. The Montreal Conference of 1989 succeeded in obtaining a general agreement on the nature of the problem and on its solution, namely the development and use of alternative propellants that are ozone-harmless. As a result, the use of CFCs will cease in the industrialized countries, and research and development to this end are being actively pursued. The difficulty is that some of the poorer countries, such as India and China, have recently started up CFC manufacture in response to the national need for extending refrigeration rights. It is difficult to expect such countries to abandon recent investment and start again without external compensation, and this problem has not yet been solved.

- Most menacing macropollution by far: the so-called greenhouse effect, [11] which regulates the temperature

---

[11]Although the "greenhouse effect" is still under controversy and absolute certainty regarding it will not be obtained for another ten

on the earth's surface. This effect concerns the extent to which certain constituents of the atmosphere restrict the reflection of solar radiations from the surface of the earth into outer space, thus trapping the heat. The proportions of the main gases of the air, oxygen and nitrogen, seem to have remained constant during millennia, and all life processes are regulated by this. However, other gases which exist in much smaller concentration and were formerly referred to as trace gases control the greenhouse effect. Since the Industrial Revolution the concentration of these gases has increased. The most important of these, carbon dioxide, has increased by 25%, oxides of nitrogen by 19% and methane by 100%. In addition, newcomers to the atmosphere such as our notorious, manmade CFCs also add to the effect as does terrestrial ozone. Concern with the consequences of greenhouse-effect changes arose from observations of the increase in carbon dioxide concentration. Realization of the influence of the other trace gases came quite recently. It was noticed that the concentration of CO_2 in the atmosphere, although small, had been increasing. Indeed CO_2 concentration in the atmosphere has increased more since the Industrial Revolution than in the previous 16,000 years owing to the combustion of fossil fuels such as oil and coal which are the basis of industrialization. The increase also results from a reduction of Nature's capacity to absorb the gas through photosynthesis in the green leaf, as a result of the extensive elimination of the tropical forests.

A number of different and highly sophisticated global climatic models indicate that a doubling of the previ-

years, by that time, if—as it is highly likely—it is confirmed, it will be too late to do anything about it.

ous equilibrium concentration of CO_2 would result in an average increase in the surface temperature of the planet of between 1.5° and 4.5° Celsius. It is extremely difficult for the world public to appreciate that this invisible and apparently harmless gas, which bubbles up from our whiskey and soda or Coca-Cola and which we ourselves exhale, is a potential eliminator of our prosperity and life-style. Assuming the continuation of present industrial practices in the burning of fossil fuels, saturation might be reached in forty to forty-five years. Increasing concentration of the other greenhouse gases makes the problem still more imminent.

Great uncertainties still exist with regard to this problem, especially concerning the role of the oceans in absorbing carbon dioxide and the possible existence of other "sinks" for the gas. However, circumstantial evidence is now so strong that the probability has to be taken seriously. The probable consequences of Earth warming will be discussed in the next chapter. Suffice it to say here that they are many and serious. This becomes, therefore, a classic case of the need to develop methods of management and decision making within uncertainty. If the nations avoid taking action until the consequences of the greenhouse effect become incontestably obvious, it may be too late to stop it, with disastrous results. On the other hand, if action is taken now and the onset is slower than predicted, enormous costs will have been incurred.

We must return briefly to the question of the elimination of the forests, which, in addition to its contribution to the greenhouse effect, is to be deprecated for many other reasons. It generates local and regional climatic changes, causes soil erosion and downstream flooding, and frequently leaves soils which are unable to carry a sustained agriculture. Especially in the case of the Amazon Basin, it involves the extinction of innumerable plant and animal species at a time when the preservation of genetic diversity is of immense importance. In addition, great human suffering and cultural loss is created as forest peoples are displaced or eliminated.

We must mention also the problem of the increasing scarcity of fuelwood in many countries of Africa, in Asia, and elsewhere. The burning of wood and charcoal still remains the main domestic energy source for a great proportion of populations, especially those in rural areas. The gathering of wood is generally a woman's task. With demographic growth accessible, wood becomes increasingly scarce, and in some cases a task that used to take a couple of hours a day now demands six. Shortage of wood encourages rural populations to burn animal dung, which results in loss of nitrogen to sustain crops and deterioration of the soil. In many tropical cities the cost of fuelwood has become exorbitant, and households turn to kerosene for domestic needs, thus necessitating the use of scarce foreign currency, as does changing food habits. As Lester Brown[12] puts it, many cities in the poorer countries are "living from ship to mouth."

[12]President of the Worldwatch Institute, Washington, D.C.

THE ADVANCE OF HIGH TECHNOLOGIES

Our present society is built materially on highly successful technological development. Ever since the onset of the Industrial Revolution, with its replacement of human and animal power, first by the steam engine and later by electricity, manpower productivity has mounted. Despite early fears, this has led to increased markets, increased employments and a spreading of prosperity. At first, these developments were mainly based on empirical invention. With the arising of the chemical and electrical industries, however, the main impulse to development has come from the discoveries of the scientific laboratories. The success of technological development and of application of the scientific method in determining the outcome of the Second World War led postwar governments and their industries to give massive resource support to scientific research and its application in technology. The lead time from scientific discovery through applied research and technical development to production is long, hence during the first part of the period under review we saw mainly improvements and novelties of a relatively traditional type. Later, breakthrough and utterly new types of technology appeared, especially from the discoveries of solid-state physics and molecular biology.

The applications of the new, advanced technologies are so widespread that we can present here only a very superficial indication of their significance.

The ubiquitous application of microelectronics is most obvious in factories, offices, and shops. The silicon-chip microprocessor with its low cost and extreme miniaturization makes it possible to provide a brain and a memory for any piece of equipment humanly devised. Furthermore, microelectronic techniques articulate well with many other types of advanced technology, such as holography, satellites, liquid crystal techniques and glass-fibre optics. The results appear in an enormous variety of microelectronic devices and gadgets. Computers first developed during the war and bulkily filling whole rooms with their equipment are now miniaturized, much faster, more reliable, cheaper and diffused everywhere.

Microelectronics have penetrated deeply into industry at every stage from design to packaging. Automation and robotization are modifying industrial processes and structures, and are eliminating dangerous, dirty and repetitive jobs, creating the need for new skills and challenging educational and training traditions. And this is only a beginning; new generations of "smart robots" are appearing which can see and feel; emphasis is changing from improvements in line-production towards integrated systems of manufacture; new types of equipment are being devised through mechatronics, a combined approach which brings together electronic and advanced mechanical techniques. These advances are rapidly penetrating all sectors of the economy and constitute the basis of the postindustrial society. Whether this will be fully realized or not depends on the evolution of many of the other changes we have described.

Automatic banking and the cashless society are already there, while automated Stock Exchanges and financial transfer systems operate at times all too quickly; the computer has invaded every type of research activity from history to aircraft design.

Nowhere has the impact of electronics been more marked than in communications. Telephone systems have improved immeasurably. The use of telefax has spread at an extraordinary rate in a remarkably short period of time; electronic mail systems proliferate and video-conferencing is possible. Most dramatic of all has been the steadily advancing influence of television. This powerful extension of the media has extended worldwide during our period; it is employed for the conditioning of populations to accept the acts of dictators, for educational purposes, for the broadcasting of news and opinions often with distortion and trivialization and, above all, for entertainment. Its influence on the political system is now enormous. Elections are swayed by projections of the charisma or its absence by the candidates. On the other hand, live transmission of parliamentary proceedings has, in a number of countries, exposed the triviality of debate and the banality of political personalities. This has contributed to the present loss of public confidence in the operation of the democratic system by demonstrating the contrived confrontation of vote-seeking political parties.

A word must be added concerning the significance of the other main line of advancing technology, namely in a biology transformed by the understanding of the functions of DNA, the unravelling of the genetic code and the other discoveries of molecular biology. These developments are much less visible to the public than those of microelectronics, but are equally profound and important for the human future. Many difficult ethical problems have surfaced, especially with regard to the potential manipulation of human genes. Already genetic engineering has produced many important advances in medicine, and many more are to be expected. Great advances have been made to the modification of plant and animal species in the direction of protection against diseases and changes of climate, as well as increasing production and modifying the product. Thus dramatic genetic modifications are likely to produce considerable increases in milk yields, initially at least, in places where there are already abundant lakes of milk. It is somewhat troublesome to note that recent judgments make it possible to obtain patent rights for new genetically produced species.

WORLD FINANCE

The economic transformation of the Eastern European countries, including the Soviet Union, necessitates quick and rapid action if economic collapse is to be avoided. Rejection of the Marxist system and conversion to a market economy is not easy. Not only do new structures have to be created, but entirely changed attitudes on the part of work forces and management are necessary for adaptation to a competitive system. Guaranteed employment in the old system inevitably meant low productivity, while lack of incentive inhibited all innovation. As a consequence, these countries find themselves edging towards a competitive situation with large debts, obsolete and highly polluting factories with outdated equipment, shortage of capital and a lack of modern management skills. Social and psychological adjustment will be necessary, for example, in facing the unfamiliar situation of massive unemployment. Great help will be needed from outside, not only in the provision of capital but also in the form of technical and managerial assistance and many other aspects of free market development. In the case of unified Germany, the Federal Republic will be able to furnish capital, managerial capacity and training, but it is unlikely that the transformation of the East will be achieved without considerable individual and social hardship.

Great hopes have been raised in Eastern Europe with regard to the prosperity that will flow from the adoption of the market economy. While these are largely justified, at least in the longer term, it is important that the market forces not be regarded as the unique agent for the acquisition of a better life and that their limits be well understood as mentioned earlier. It is necessary not to cast ideals out indiscriminately and to retain some of the more positive aspects of socialism. Otherwise there could be a backlash against capitalism.

Political power in the modern world is no longer controlled mainly by the power and relative sophistication of armaments but is increasingly determined by financial power. Indeed in recent history excessive expenditure on armaments has proved ruinous to the two superpowers, while the two countries prevented from rearming after defeat in the Second World War are those with the largest surpluses. In addition, it is detrimental for the big powers that their industries depend only on the state market and do not therefore obey the normal free trading conditions such as they exist in other industries.

In the mid-to-late 1980s financial frenzy gripped the world markets. Financial and currency-exchange speculation aided by computerized communications became a game utterly outside economic reality. Mergers between firms aimed at immediate gains and unrelated to long-term efficiency mushroomed. Insider trading and other forms of corruption flourished in places hitherto regarded as ethically reliable. Economic gain was conceived in terms of financial transactions rather than of innovative and competitive development, often in isolation from the physical reality underlying finance (oil price determined by the action of cartels rather than on the availability of oil, ease of extraction, etc.). The consequences of such practices gave rise to fears of stock market collapse; they also represented a flight from real industry to financial folly. Financial instability is still a serious point of turbulence within the problematique, even if reality has come home to roost, with many financial geniuses either in prison or bankrupt.

The Loss of Values

There appears to be a general loss of the values which previously ensured the coherence of society and the conformity of its individuals. In some places this has been the result of a loss of faith in religion and the ethical values it promulgates. In other cases it stems from a loss of confidence in the political system and those who operate it. Yet again, the welfare state, despite all the social advantages and security it brings, seems to have reduced the sense of responsibility and self-reliance of many individuals. This has led to an increasing rejection by minorities of the decisions of the majority, often reinforced by a sense of social injustice or exploitation. However, there is in the meanwhile a lot of caring and good organisation to help those who need help. These signs remain still modest.

These and many other causes have led to the lack of social discipline, to vandalism and violence that have become a trademark of our age. In cases of real or imagined political persecution or racial discrimination, violence can breed terrorism, which attracts the energies of disgruntled people and fanatics. Such groups have taken advantage of technology that provides them with new and effective explosives, accurate timing-delay devices and remote triggering. In some cases, terrorist and sabotage training and supplies may have been provided by rogue countries. These are all manifestations of the general malaise of contemporary society that can in fact be dealt with as such in cases where deep injustice is the cause.

THE NEW PLAGUES

A different category is that of crime, violence and coercion organised for monetary gain or political power. The classic case is that of the Mafia. Still more dangerous has been the emergence in recent years of a well-organised and ruthless drug trade—through mafias and other similar groups—that has gained enormous power and attacks whole governments with its terrorist tactics. It is said that the totality of the drug trade exceeds even that of the oil industry. The drug network, from the grower through the drug barons who operate chemical plants for refining and conversion, to the couriers and distributors, is all-pervasive and at times seems invulnerable. The human misery and disintegration caused is enormous, and as we are about to indicate, it spreads lethal disease. The growth of this evil, which shows no sign of slowing down, has become a subject of deep concern, but there is great uncertainty about how to attack it. The best solution would be to abolish demand through treatment and education, but this is very difficult in view of the wide dispersion of drugtakers, so attempts are being made to eliminate power centres of the industry and compensate the growers to allow them to produce food crops.

Finally, we must point out the recently appeared and deadly disease known as AIDS. Triggered by the HIV virus, it is a sexually transmitted disease which is also passed on by drug users through contaminated needles. Furthermore, contaminated pregnant women have a very high chance of giving birth to babies who will carry and probably develop the virus. Also, in the early stages of its history, the virus was transmitted to receivers of blood transfusions in which the donated blood had not been checked for the virus. An infected person may carry the virus for a number of years without any illness, but then the virus usually develops into AIDS, which attacks the immune system and causes death by means of one of the many diseases that the patient is unable to fight because of a damaged immune system. At present, progress has been made towards a cure, and new treatments aimed at alleviation or extension of life are being tested with encouraging signs.

Already AIDS appears to have reached pandemic proportions in some African countries, and its spread globally is greatly feared. Apart from the mortality and terrible human suffering involved, the cost of treatment and education campaigns is a tremendous burden for countries in which AIDS is rife, monopolising hospital accommodations and diverting attention and effort from the cure or control of malaria, bilharzia and other debilitating diseases.

At a time when medicine has made such extraordinary progress both in its therapeutic and its preventive capacities, AIDS reminds us that in spite of all this progress, man remains vulnerable in the area of health, both physically and mentally. This deadly disease, along with the mutation of certain viruses that make vaccination ineffective, demonstrates that at least for the time being, the permanent struggle for human health can no more be avoided than death itself, despite some wishful thinking.

II

SOME AREAS OF
ACUTE CONCERN

FROM OUR SURVEY OF RECENT CHANGE, IT IS clear how extensive the interactions among the various elements are. Population growth in a poor country, for instance, means that more food has to be grown, which in turn puts pressure on soil and water resources. If food has to be imported, it means the diversion of scarce hard-currency reserves from other forms of development. Again, the larger population will have an impact on the environment, leading perhaps to excessive cutting of trees for fuel, with the social consequences that we have described.

This chapter will deal with some of the most urgent of the material problems that now appear to be threatening humanity, and especially that part of the problematique consisting of the intertwining factors of *population, environment, food* and *energy.*

THE GROWTH OF HUMAN ACTIVITY

A central feature of the global situation is the enormous increase in the totality of human activity during the present century, which has necessarily led to a huge rise in the demand for raw materials and energy. Much of this increase is due, of course, to the spectacular growth of the world population during this period, which will be added to in the years to come by cohort after cohort of new inhabitants to our planet. Some people[1] argue that fertility has begun to decrease in all parts of the world. According to United Nations estimates, the level of fertility has gone from an average of 6.1 children per woman in 1965–1970 to 3.9 in 1985. The demographic mutation is therefore general. The cultural obstacles to demographic change are considerable, and they can delay the expected evolutions by one or two decades, but they can do no more in the end than slow down an inevitable trend, which is largely attributable to modernization. The issue is not whether fertility will go down but when and at what rate.

All the same, even if fertility were to slow down drastically, the demographic thrust contained in the age-pyramid is still such that the population growth will continue on its course for many decades to come, and this will require some very audacious development strategies.

But there is an even more powerful factor in the growth of human activity, namely the increased consumption per capita that economic growth has made

[1]Chesnais, 1987.

possible and that has reciprocally been a cause of that growth.

As evidenced by the proliferation of mass-produced goods spawned by the factories of the industrialized world, we live in a consumption society. In Europe, before the Industrial Revolution, consumption per capita was little different from that of many of the less-developed countries today. Now the average per capita consumption of materials and energy is about forty times greater in the North than in the less developed countries. At the extreme the disparity may be more than 100:1. This is not only a reflection of social injustice but an indication of the upscaling of our exploitation of Nature.

Compounding population numbers with average per capita consumption gives a rough indication of the totality of human activity. We estimate that this may have increased some fortyfold over the century. Until now, consumption in the rich countries has been the main component of this burgeoning activity, but in the coming decades the demographic component will become increasingly important.

Into this picture of resource consumption we must sketch the criminally wasteful use of resources—human, material and energy—consumed for military purposes as a source of work and profit for some developed countries. It is difficult to understand how the peoples of the world have been willing to tolerate such waste in the face of extensive hunger, poverty, disease and underdevelopment, which themselves breed war and violence. It is not easy to be precise with regard to the magnitude of military resource consumption. National financial expenditures on defence do, however, give some indication. Its recent world total appears to have been of the order of about U.S. $1 trillion in real terms, a fourfold increase since the end of the Second World War and a twenty-five-fold escalation since the beginning of the century. Figures of this magnitude are not easy to appreciate in perspective, so some comparisons may be useful. It has been pointed out, for instance, that for many years the military expenditure of the world has been comparable with the combined GNPs (Gross National Product) of all the countries of Latin America and Africa together. The annual budget of UNICEF[2] is equivalent to about four hours of world military cost. The elimination of smallpox under WHO[3] guidance took ten years to achieve and cost under $100 million in U.S. dollars, less than the cost of developing a small air-to-air missile. We can only hope that this waste of resources will now be reduced considerably as a result of extensive disarmament—and that the savings will be diverted to the essential and constructive needs of the underprivileged.

Consideration of resource consumption and its disparities brings us to the concept of sustainable development which was so clearly and optimistically expounded in the Brundtland Report[4] on environment and sustainable development. It is doubtful that a global sustainable development can be achieved with the growth rate in the industrialized countries increasing at the rate suggested in the report. A sustainable society implicitly connotes one that is based

[2]United Nations International Children Emergency Fund.
[3]World Health Organisation.
[4]World Commission on Environment and Development, 1987.

on a long-term vision in that it must foresee the consequences of its diverse activities to ensure that they do not break the cycles of renewal; it has to be a society of conservation and generational concern. It must avoid the adoption of mutually irreconcilable objectives. Equally, it must be a society of social justice because great disparities of wealth or privilege will breed destructive disharmony. In other words, the concept is utopian but one well worth striving for. The sustainable society would never arise within a world economy which relied *exclusively* on the operation of the market forces, important as these may be, for the maintenance of vitality and creative innovation. As we mentioned earlier, market forces respond uniquely to very short-term signals and are no sure guide to longer-term considerations.

Accepting, therefore, the concept of sustainability, one has to inquire about the general level of material affluence that can be sustained and the disparities between the richer and the poorer—both within and between countries—that can be tolerated, taking into account social justice as well as practical realities. This is no plea for egalitarianism; indeed, collective values in recent years have preached a pseudoegalitarianism that inevitably collided with the realities of human nature.

In seeking a normative approach to future world development at this moment of turbulence and change, it is vital to discover whether the present levels of material prosperity in the rich industrialized countries are compatible with global sustainability or, better perhaps, whether a world economy driven by stimulated consumer demand can continue for long.

This is particularly pertinent in the face of population and environmental constraints. It is, of course, a controversial question which few if any governments would have the courage to face. But it is the vital question of the present, and will eventually be forced on the politicians by the people. We believe that consumerism in its present form cannot persist, not only because of the constraints but also because of the deeper reasons of human values. The shallow satisfactions of consumerism—"keeping up with the Joneses" and "I am what I own"—are incompatible with a decent human life, which needs a deep sense of self. It leads through greed to many manifestations of the "malaise," which we will describe later.[5]

Here we must stress that we are not advocating zero economic growth. Indeed, we are convinced of the need to stimulate growth in the underdeveloped South, but for the industrialized North with the evolution of the postindustrial society, the need seems to be more for growth of quality.

GLOBAL WARMING AND ITS ENERGY IMPLICATIONS

At the present state of our knowledge of the complex interactions within the planetary system, the greenhouse effect appears to be the most imminent of the constraints to the extension, or perhaps even to the survival, of an economic approach that has served richer countries well for so long. The consequences of the heating up of the earth's surface cannot yet be sensed with any degree of precision, but there seems to be agreement about the general trends.

[5]See Chapter 6.

"We've always thought of climate as an act of God. It requires an enormous shift in the way we think of the world and our place in it to understand that we have already moved into an era in which we are actually responsible for managing climatic parameters. Finally, after years of mistakes, we are coming to recognize that continued economic prosperity is tied to ecological stewardship. There is responsible profit to be made in caring for the planet."

> Robert Redford,
> Founder of Institute for
> Resource Management in
> Greenhouse Glasnost*

The range of estimated rises in temperature from a doubling of the equilibrium CO_2 concentration is considerably greater than cyclical changes which have appeared in historical times. The effect will not be uniform over the surface of the earth. It will be small at the equator and much greater at high latitudes. This will alter the thermal gradients of the planet and is expected to change the pattern of precipitation considerably, modifying the various climatic zones and hence their viability for agriculture. It is expected, for example, that major food-producing areas such as the bread bowls of the American Middle West and the Ukraine will become arid, whereas other areas to the North will become fertile. Transitions may or may not be gradual, but in either

* The Sundance Summit on Global Climate Change (Sundance, Utah, 1989).

case world food security becomes of great concern. We are also told to expect less regular climatic conditions than in the past and more numerous extremes, with a greater frequency of hurricanes. Indeed, one of the greatest sources of uncertainty in predicting local and global climate change is the effect that the warming will have on cloud coverage. The monsoon cloud system of the tropics, for example, is a main factor of climate regulation, and it is known that it reacts significantly to small changes in ocean temperature.

A further consequence of the heating would be a rise in sea level, resulting from thermal expansion of the waters and run-off from landborne ice. This might mean a general rise of the sea level of as much as one metre, leading to the submerging of low-level regions and exposure of larger areas to the danger of flooding at spring tides and storms. Of course, the sea-level rise would take place gradually over the years, so there should be time for adjustment. The effect would virtually eliminate some groups of islands and greatly erode many important river deltas, such as those of the Nile and the Ganges, and displace large populations. It is interesting to realize that over the last one hundred years, the global sea level has risen 10–20 cm, while the mean surface air temperature has increased by about 0.5° Celsius.

There are, of course, many measures which can be taken to delay and buffer the earth-heating and eventually to bring it to a halt. The fundamental need is to reduce carbon dioxide emission by massively reducing the combustion of fossil fuels. The 1988 Toronto Conference of scientists suggested that it would be necessary to reduce CO_2 emission by some 20% by 2005. Some valuable years of grace could be won through a worldwide campaign of energy conservation and efficiency. Some argue persuasively that intensive attack on energy efficiency could itself solve the problem. However, even if this should be so, the long lead-time in the development of the new efficient processes makes it unlikely that the exclusive reliance on such a policy would enable control of the warming quickly enough. Increasing energy efficiency and conservation as well as the development of soft energy sources must be the immediate task if disruption of industrial production and individual hardship are to be avoided.

What then are the energy prospects? While there is a present glut of oil, we are nearing the end of the long period during which this nonrenewable resource has been cheap and plentiful. Quite apart then from the need to reduce its use as primary fuel because of the greenhouse effect, measures should gradually be instituted to conserve this vital resource as a feedstock for the petrochemical industry that will be required indefinitely for the production of plastics, pharmaceuticals, dyestuffs and a host of other products now assumed to be essential. There is still coal in plenty, but it seems as if it is becoming too dangerous to use because of earth-warming, unless the technological progress currently taking place makes it possible to considerably limit its negative effects. Soft energy alternatives, such as solar, wind, tidal and geothermal, can be provided no doubt, but at the present rates of development they are unlikely to be available in sufficient quantities in time to compensate for the necessary reduction in the use of fossil fuels. Present estimates suggest that the soft sources may be providing some 8–10% of world energy needs at the end of the century. Apparently, prospects are good for great improvement in the efficiency of photovoltaic cells, but the vision of their covering vast areas of land, which would then not be usable for other purposes, is hardly attractive.

The promise of nuclear fusion has been held out for many years as the eventual and virtually inexhaustible solution to all our energy problems. This may prove true, but its abundant availability seems to be as far off as when the idea was first propounded. We can certainly not rely on fusion to fill the gap if and when earth-warming forces us to reduce the use of fossil fuels.

It appears that we may have to prepare for a critical situation to arise a few decades ahead, when we are forced by the dangers of earth-warming to drastically reduce our use of fossil fuels and will have no alternatives in sight. In such circumstances nuclear fission could be the only possibility of partial alleviation of the situation. Many of us have been unhappy for a long time at the proliferation of nuclear power stations with their obvious dangers as well as those of storage of nuclear waste, but we now reluctantly admit that the use of coal and oil is probably more dangerous to society, because of the carbon dioxide they produce, than is nuclear. There are therefore strong arguments for keeping the nuclear option open and for the development of fast breeder reactors. We must warn, however, that the adoption of this option could only provide a fractional solution. It would be almost impossible to make available the capital and the effort for the construction of sufficient nuclear power stations in time to match what will probably be the necessary reduction of carbon dioxide.

The impact of earth-warming would be particularly difficult for the poorer countries. Development demands energy for industry and agriculture as well as for meeting the domestic requirements of increasing populations. The type of situation which might arise is illustrated dramatically by the industrialization intentions of China, the most populous country of the world. These are based on the use of coal, of which the country has large reserves, and would eventually make China one of the leading countries of the world in carbon dioxide pollution at a time when the rest of the world's industry was striving to drastically reduce its emission. To force China or for that matter any developing country to halt its industrialization without compensation would be morally wrong, politically disastrous and practically impossible. The Chinese experts are well aware of this problem, but the dilemma will not go away.

GLOBAL FOOD SECURITY

Production of sufficient food to meet the needs of a rapidly increasing world population is obviously a matter of primary concern. In the early 1970s when the significance of the population explosion first received general attention, authoritative voices assured us that it should be possible to grow food for a world population as high as 20 billion. This is probably technically so, if agriculture is considered in isolation. In the real world, however, it has to be considered in terms of the problematique because of constraints due to other factors. For example, in the long-term estimates of food production possibilities, it was assumed that water-shortages could be overcome by desalination of brackish waters or of sea water through technological innovations which demand pressure would conjure up. This took no account of the enormous energy requirements which would be needed for such processes, nor for the availability of the energy.

Nevertheless, the success of agricultural production since the end of the Second World War has been phenomenal and has led to a situation of considerable world surplus, despite demographic growth. In 1987 it was estimated that world food production was sufficient to provide some 19% more calories than was necessary to provide a reasonable diet for every person on earth. Yet vast areas of hunger and malnutrition persisted, worsened by drought, famine and warfare. It seems, therefore, that the existence of plenty of food in the world has little relevance to the persistence of hunger. The success of the Green Revolution in India in transforming from food deficit to surplus, for example, does not seem to have eliminated hunger in that country. The hungry are the poor, unable to buy the food that exists, so that hunger in large areas of the world is but a symptom of the basic problem of poverty. It is true that more people are being fed adequately today than in our base year of 1968; nevertheless, in absolute terms hunger continues to grow.

The co-existence of glut and famine seems intolerable and gives rise to problems in the surplus as well as in the deficit countries. In the former, difficulties related to surpluses, subsidies and the needs of the farmers are formidable. The greatest food reserves, available for export, exist in North America, with the deficit countries depending on the success of its harvests. Given the continuation of the present patterns of agricultural production, the main deficit areas at the end of the century will be the Middle East and North Africa and also in Sub-Saharan Africa, where a shortfall of 60 million tons of cereals per annum is estimated.

But will the patterns persist? The droughts of 1988 sent a shock throughout the world food system. The drought in the United States appears to have been the most severe ever recorded, with grain production falling below domestic consumption for the first time. The U.S. harvest fell by 31% and that of Canada by 27%. The deficits were made good by drawing from accumulated stocks, from which also export contracts with some 100 countries that depend on food imports from North America were respected. This led to a dramatic fall in world food reserves. The question arises as to what would happen if similar droughts were to recur frequently. It is premature to attribute the 1988 drought, which also affected many other parts of the world, to global warming, but the event was a clear warning of the vulnerability of food security to changes of climate.

Until about 1950, increase in agricultural production came mainly from the extension of land under cultivation. Thereafter, massive expansion was achieved through the use of chemical fertilizers. Thus agriculture no longer depends solely on current solar energy, but relies considerably on fossil fuels—the stored solar energy of past aeons.

It takes approximately a ton of oil or its equivalent in natural gas to produce a ton of nitrogenous fertilizer. Petroleum is also necessary for the manufacture of weed killers and pesticides which are used extensively in modern agriculture, as well as for tillage and the operation of irrigation pumps. During the period 1950–1986, the average consumption of fertilizers per inhabitant of the planet rose from 5 to 26 Kg while at the same time the area per capita devoted to cereals dropped from 0.24 to 0.15 hectares. This means that, in a crude sense, the great increase in world food production represents the conversion of oil into edible cereals via the photosynthetic process. Agriculture in the traditional sense hardly exists in many parts of the world. It has become a sector of industry, relying on technological innovation and modern management methods like any other sector. Likewise, agriculture as both user and producer of energy has to be considered as an element of the world energy system. Future scarcity or high cost of oil, or constraints to its use forced by global warming, would inhibit the production of food and greatly raise food prices at a time when continuing high population growth will demand more and more food. It is certainly desirable to reduce the energy intensity of agriculture, but much hard thinking is necessary to ascertain the extent to which "organic farming" could indeed provide the food needs for present and future populations.

Another potential danger to agricultural sustainability is a widespread degradation and erosion of soil. Soil erosion is a natural process, but when its rate exceeds that of new soil formation, there is a decline in the fertility of the land. It is estimated that this is the situation in some 35% of the world's croplands. In areas of drought and overpopulation of humans or animals and in many regions such as the

> In Mexico, according to information provided by
> the Xochicalli Foundation, 19,000 k/cal have to be
> used in order to put 2,200 k/cal of food on the ta-
> ble. From another angle the amount of energy con-
> sumed in transporting foodstuffs in Mexico is
> almost equal to the total energy required by the
> primary sector for food production. The fact that
> such situations are considered to be positive is, un-
> doubtedly, a conceptual aberration.
>
> Manfred Max-Neef
> in Human Scale for Development
> CEPAUR—Dag Hammarskjöld Foundation

Sahel in Africa, recent years have witnessed marginal
arable land turning to an arid rangeland and then to
desert. In the case of the North American bread bas-
ket, unsuitable soils have been forced into production
and good soils "mined" to meet the ever-increasing
demand for food from outside. Enormous amounts of
fertile topsoil are washed away by the rains, into the
rivers.

Intensive agricultural practices such as those of the
Green Revolution demand much more use of water
than do the traditional methods. As a result, ground-
water levels are falling in many areas, throwing
doubt as to the long-term sustainability of the practices. Increased use of irrigation has also greatly
added to the use of water in many places, often with
spectacular results. But it has often led to salination
of the soils with destruction of their fertility. This is,
however, only one element in the approaching crisis
in global water availability. Domestic demand for water increases rapidly as economic growth is achieved.

Then many industrial technologies require vast amounts of water. Acute water problems result from the growth of the cities, especially those built in arid regions, unsuited by Nature to carry large urban populations. Finally, we must stress again the imminent danger of contamination of the aquifers by the diffusion of toxic and radioactive wastes.

Special mention should be made of some of the distortions caused by the penetration of Western styles and needs into some of the developing countries. In many places, and especially in the African cities, food habits have been transformed, partly owing to the availability of famine-relief or low-priced food imports. Thus bread has become popular in areas not suitable for wheat farming and rice is greatly in favour despite the high water-needs for its cultivation. This tendency is much to the detriment of traditional food crops and reduces incentives to the farmers to raise production. While the production of plantation crops in continuation of the practices of colonial times is useful in earning foreign currency, if carried to excess in countries with insufficient food for domestic consumption, it is obviously unwise. This is especially the case where large areas are devoted to the growing of cattle feeds for use in the food-saturated West . . . often as pet food.

THE POPULATION BACKLASH

The longer-term consequences of demographic change are inextricably related to future world development and harmony. The industrialized countries with their aging populations, automation and the considerable productivity increase that it will generate, should go some way towards maintaining living standards with a reduced work force. However, the substantial increase of elderly people will throw a great burden on the pension funds and on the health and welfare systems. Some of these countries are turning to pronatalist policies, but as yet, with little success. Considerable structural adjustments will have to be made in these countries in view of shrinking intake to the educational system and the extension of health and welfare services for the elderly, compensated partly by a lightened burden for child health needs. Although a smaller proportion of the population will be within the formal learning system great efforts will have to be made to increase its quality and depth: success in the postindustrial society will depend critically on the quality of human resource development. Flexible and selective means will have to be found for late retirement to make available the skills of older people still capable of contributing significantly to society. The "age-imbalance" problem can be regarded as a sign of success in family planning. It is a temporary phenomenon and can be planned for in advance. In Sweden where these problems were first recognized, the situation is now in balance.

For the less-developed countries, the problems are quite the opposite. In most instances, growth of the economy and elimination of poverty will have to be the main objectives: this means a type of growth that respects and is built on the traditional cultures rather than being a slavish imitation of the materialist growth of the North, which would inevitably induce the same malaise from which the industrialized countries now suffer. But too great a population increase can be a fatal constraint to development. In many cases already, development plans are unrealistic because of insufficient weight being given to this factor.

Here, however we are more concerned about the progression of the North–South demographic disparities. By the middle of the next century, inhabitants of the presently industrialized countries will constitute well under 20% of the world population. Can we envisage a future world with a ghetto of rich nations, armed with sophisticated weapons to protect themselves against the hoards of hungry, uneducated, unemployed and very angry people outside. Such a scenario, which is a projection from present trends, is unlikely. Presently unforeseeable world events will surely intervene and also, by that time, several of the less-developed countries will no doubt possess their own nuclear weapons.

More likely, population pressures, opportunity gradients and conditions of tyranny and oppression will have generated waves of migration towards the North and the West, which it will be impossible to contain. Our successors are likely to see mass migrations on an unprecedented scale. Such movements have already begun, with the "boat-people" of the Far East, Mexicans slipping over the border into the United States and Asians and Africans to Europe. At the extreme it is not difficult to imagine innumerable immigrants landing from their boats on the Northern shores of the Mediterranean and consisting of the hungry and the desperate. Similarly, massive emigration from Latin America to the United States is to be expected, while population pressure in China may seek relief by entering an empty Siberia. As we have already suggested, rising of the sea level as a result of the greenhouse effect could greatly increase migration pressures, for example, in Bangladesh and Egypt.

It is therefore urgent to improve the economic conditions in the poor countries, and at the same time to introduce effective means of population control. We would like to stress that reductions in economic disparity and aid to development of a wise and co-operative character, far from being a humanitarian gesture is of fundamental self-interest to the rich countries. This is little understood by the general public in the industrialized countries and, until it is, the politicians are unlikely to act. Nevertheless, it is clear that no measures will effectively stop the immigration trends. This could induce a sharp rise in defensive racism in the receiving countries and encourage the emergence of a series of right-wing dictators swept in by popular vote. Such situations must not be allowed to develop. It is therefore equally important, besides increasing aid to development in the poor countries, to prepare the populations of the rich countries to accept this reality.

The Information Society

The emergence of the Information or Post-Industrial Society is one of the main agents of planetary change. If wisely guided and its problems are tackled in time, this development can make possible so many improvements to the human condition. We have already described the development of microelectronics and how its applications are penetrating into every aspect of everyday and industrial life. Here we are concerned with its economic, social and political consequences.

The developments on which the information society is based were made mainly in the scientific and industrial laboratories of the countries of the North; inevitably, the revolutionary applications of microelectronics have flooded the markets of the industrialized countries. Our discussion of consequences therefore has a strongly "Northern" flavour. As yet, there has been much less direct impact in the developing countries. Nevertheless the significance of these innovations to the development of the South both for better and for worse is as we shall see later, very great.

The rapid development of microelectronics with its integrated circuits in which the silicon chip may contain a million electronical elements, took place mainly in the United States and in Japan. In the former, most of the research and development was undertaken in the laboratories of relatively small, sophisticated firms (Silicon Valley) under contracts from the defence department and the space agency. In Japan it was made possible by co-operation between the large electrical enterprises and the government as part of an imaginative long-term strategy. The Europeans entered the field at a later stage and are making great, but possibly insufficient efforts to catch up. Competition in this area is particularly rugged.

It must be stressed at the outset that the coming of the postindustrial society does not mean that products, including those of heavy industry, will become less necessary, as some facile public statements seem to imply. Those engaged in information-handling in the future will still require housing, knives and forks and plates, as well as food on their plates. There will probably be less commuting, as much of the computer work will be done at home. They will probably aspire to the independence given by the automobile, but, even should cars be scarce and expensive to fuel, public transport will necessitate the manufacture of buses, trains and ships. In the information society, industry will still flourish, but its products will be provided by a much smaller proportion of the work force than in the heyday of the industrial era. The majority will be in the information handling industries and the service sector, a trend that is already well advanced.

Technological development has had a strong influence on the nature and behaviour of society ever since the shaping of the first flint or bone tools. The Industrial Revolution gradually evolved to the type of society we are living in today and the advanced technologies, already modifying life-styles and creating new occupations, may have an even greater effect. The central promise of the information society through its ubiquitous applications in industry and the service sector is increased manpower productivity. It should become possible to provide all the requirements of a country—including those of industrial production, agriculture, defence, health, education and welfare—and an acceptable standard of living for everyone with only a fraction of the physical work expended today. No country will be able to ignore these developments or slow down their actualization. To do so would mean forgoing their potential benefits, as well as risking economic losses in international trade. But the extent, depth and unforeseeable social consequences of this potential make it necessary to look well beyond the present decade in an attempt to ensure their exploitation to the maximum human benefit. If this is not done and developments are planned merely on the basis of medium-term gains and on narrow vested interest, governments will try to absorb social and other consequences by marginal adjustments of existing social models and policies in an attempt to eliminate crisis situations as they become acute. It would be irresponsible to leave such developments, so fundamental to the health of society, exclusively to the operation of the market forces with their inevitably short-term signals.

It is not possible at this stage to foresee the consequences of these innovations with any clarity, but some trends are already visible. In the information society interdependence between individuals and between countries will increase through the immediate visibility of information. It will lead to a greater complexity of institutions and societies. It could enable a high degree of power and decision making, but it could equally well serve the will of unscrupulous leaders to consolidate centralized power. There will be the means for the electronic control of everyone's activities by "Big Brother" dictators and societies, far more effective than myriads of secret police.

Technological developments tend to increase the vulnerability of society, and this is particularly so as electronic devices spread. Power stations, oil refineries, nuclear reactors, communication centres and data banks all have nerve centres which are of relatively easy access to sabotage and political terrorism: these activities are themselves becoming more dangerous as they acquire more sophisticated techniques. We have already seen how the subtle injection of a computer "virus" can spread rapidly through large systems and we are aware of how an expert electronics saboteur could penetrate and hopelessly disrupt the whole international banking network.

What the deeper social and psychological consequences of the information society will be is still more difficult to discern. In a strongly technologically based culture, there will always be a dichotomy between those who understand its workings and those who merely press the buttons. It is of course not necessary to understand electronic theory in order to enjoy television. But when the microprocessor has spread to make "black boxes" out of nearly all the equipment and artifacts of life, the sophisticated know-how of those who invent and design them and create the software will have soared beyond the comprehension of the many. Then we may be faced with a sharp distinction between the few who know and the many who do not know. The emergence of a priesthood of scientists, technologists and technocrats is hardly desirable and its prevention must be one of the objectives of educational reform.

We come now to the area of controversy that dominates discussion of the information society, namely the problem of employment.[6] The attainment of full employment is still seen as a major economic and social goal, but in its consideration, the influence of automation and technological change is seldom given much weight.

There are those who argue that the upsurge of in-

[6]See Schaff and Friedrichs, 1982.

formation technology and the automation it makes possible will follow the tradition of earlier innovations in creating new products, new industries and new markets, hence generating economic growth. This will provide replacement employment for those shed by industries with shrinking labour requirements. Others feel that the situation is inherently different from earlier technological developments and that we are likely to see economic growth without substantial job creation.

This question must be seen, not only with regard to possible job redundancies, but also with regard to the general malaise of societies. In the industrialized countries, innumerable individuals find little satisfaction in their work, even where they are liberated from the crude struggle for existence by the bounties of the welfare state. These people often give in to a sense of uselessness—uselessness to society and to themselves. Human dignity and a sense of self and purpose are basic human needs which are difficult to provide in the industrial and urban milieu and the lack of them would spread if large-scale structural unemployment were to arise.

It is evident that extensive automation in the manufacturing industry is bound to cause many redundancies, especially of unskilled manual workers; it is equally clear that as the new technologies spread, new industries will arise, providing new jobs, many of which will demand new skills. The balance between these two movements is the critical question. Over a long period it does seem certain that the labour required for the efficient operation of industry will be greatly reduced unless new markets can be found. Markets for many goods in the affluent parts of the world are approaching saturation, so substantial expansion can only be expected if the populations of the developing regions can develop to become a mass market for capital and consumer goods. This, unfortunately, seems improbable in the near future.

It is argued that a massive redundancy from the manufacturing industry would be mopped up by an expanding service sector. The analogy here is with the decline over two centuries of the proportion of the active workforce engaged in agriculture in the advanced countries to as low as 4%. This was made possible by a decrease in manpower on the farm due to mechanization. But migration from the land did not cause unemployment as the growing industrial sector was able to absorb the rural redundancies. Historical analogies can be misleading when the circumstances are not exactly parallel, and that is the case with the present transition because industrial and service sectors are automating simultaneously. It is highly improbable that the labour set free by industry as automation advances can be absorbed by the service sector as it is today. Rather, we must expect to see, as the information society evolves, a gradual coming together of productive and service functions and a combination of these in the future occupations of the average individual.

Concepts of employment, unemployment, underemployment and leisure are heavy with moral and historical values involving the work ethic and some of these words are understood pejoratively. Large numbers of people are no longer required by industry, not as a consequence of cyclical fluctuations, but because society demands and technology makes possible very high levels of manpower productivity. Then these values lose their significance and words lose their traditional meanings. It is suggested that, in the future, the chief concern of the individual may be less unemployment as we have understood it in the past, but occupation in the larger sense. It will certainly include time spent in contributing to the economic needs of society, for which he or she will be adequately paid, but also activities, self-chosen, which provide personal fulfillment. Thus the occupation of the individual will have to be seen broadly as including a proportion of intellectual or productive employment in the traditional sense. This will presumably take up a much smaller part of life (later entry, shorter hours, earlier retirement, periods off for further education and recycling), together with one or several subsidiary occupations of a craft, or educational, social, artistic or sporting activities in addition to free leisure.

Such a situation will not come about spontaneously. If thousands, and especially young people, find themselves unemployed and burdened with a seemingly endless leisure, they will be doomed to frustration. The empty time will be taken up, at best, with television viewing and playing football. More often the "pollution of leisure" will be expressed in alcoholism, drug addiction, hooliganism and delinquency. The new approach will have to be created by the will of society itself and will involve extensive changes in the educational system and in the distribution of wealth.

The above scenario is not as improbable or as radical as it may seem at first sight. If the automation of manufacturing and office work does indeed create intractable problems of unemployment and if the labour unions accept that they cannot reject the progress of automation in the face of international competition, negotiations will follow, resulting in an equitable distribution of work with shorter hours and other means. With shorter hours for all, measures will be necessary to provide socially desirable occupations on a voluntary basis. This will render the increasing extent of free time creative and satisfying, and transform the information society into the occupational society. Thus the industrialized world would be entering the golden age in which machines will work for us rather than dominate us.

This rosy picture of what could happen in the North is far from realization in the South. The developing countries are, indeed, beginning to benefit from the spread of the applications of microelectronics. Electronic communications, including those that use satellite links, are already connecting the main centres of the developing countries with those of the industrialized countries, although internal communication networks are in most cases rudimentary as a consequence of poverty.

Likewise computers are gradually filtering in, not only, as in the case of airline bookings, etc., as part of the global network, but also in the offices of governments and enterprises. However, although the advanced technologies are beginning to appear in the industries of countries such as India, Brazil and Mexico, they hardly exist in the poorer countries. This is indeed a classic example of how technological innovations inevitably favour those countries that are already advanced to the relative detriment of those at an earlier stage. In the absence of a substantial industrial infrastructure and of a capacity for science and technology, penetration of the advanced technologies is necessarily very slow.

It has been argued that rapid development in the South might be achieved by "leap-frogging" over the traditional stage of industrialization by saturating the developing countries with computers. We feel such an approach to be undesirable. In these countries unemployment and underemployment are rife. The advanced technologies are hardly labour-intensive and would create few jobs; also, they are capital-intensive and capital is a scarce commodity in the South. Furthermore, as these technologies are owned by the corporations of the North, such a scheme would induce a deep-seated technological colonialism. Nevertheless, partnership between the industrialized and the developing countries is to be encouraged highly to make sure that the latter are not forced to industrialize into the establishment of obsolete and uncompetitive economies.

The problems of environment, energy, population, food availability and development form an interpenetrating complex within the problematique which is the centre of present uncertainty concerning the human future. Because of the importance of the interactions it would make little sense to tackle each of these elements separately. To do otherwise is beyond the possibilities of the nation-state. The need is for simultaneous attack on all of them within a co-ordinated world strategy. Success or failure of the first global revolution depends essentially on this. The conflicts of the coming years will arise out of this complex of issues. Some of these have already been mentioned.

We shall only add one other example in relation to increasing scarcity of water. Some United Nations Environmental Programme (UNEP) officials feel that potential international disputes are to be foreseen with regard to the use of water from some eighteen different rivers. An acute case is the domination by Turkey of the headwaters of the Euphrates on which all Syria and a part of Iraq depend. Conflicts over these waters could very easily add one more dangerous complication to the Middle-East situation.

These matters are separately and severally under intense discussion everywhere. Conferences on earthwarming and on environmental issues in general are common. Heads of state discuss ozone-layer depletion and the greenhouse effect, but as yet no political leader has had the courage to mention the consequences in depth, nor is there any expressed acknowledgment of the interaction of the issues and the need for comprehensive attack. Political action is likely to follow only from the anguished demands of an informed public.

III

The International Mismanagement of the World Economy

Among the main areas of concern the rapid change of the world economy deserves special attention. This chapter first provides a brief and selective overview of the main issues affecting the world economy today, focused on key countries and groups of countries: the United States, Japan, the European Community, the developing countries and Eastern and Central Europe.

The U.S. Economy[1]

There are radically different views about the state of the U.S. economy, influenced by the relative importance given to different aspects of a complex situa-

[1]The following figures for the United States and Japan are official 1990 figures.

tion. This explains in part why it has proved so difficult to achieve action even on problems widely agreed to be serious such as the budget deficit.

At first sight, there are many positive elements: the U.S. economy has been growing steadily for seven years, now at an annual rate of around 2.9%. Millions of jobs have been created, and unemployment (5.2%) and inflation (4.5%) are low. GNP per capita is around U.S. $20,000, and the economy is running near capacity, at the rate of U.S. $4.13 trillion per year. From an electoral point of view, this is almost an ideal situation.

However, there is deep concern throughout the world—and among many in the United States itself —about the conditions under which this situation has been achieved, and about whether it can be sustained. For our purposes, these concerns can be grouped around four main issues that follow.

Domestic Indebtedness   In spite of repeated efforts and international commitments, the annual budget deficit continues at about U.S. $140 billion. The cumulative effect of this annual deficit is now a national debt approaching U.S. $3 trillion, risen from around U.S. $900 billion in 1981. Interest payments on this debt are now a major item in the budget, and these are evidently affected by changes in interest rates. In parallel with the growth of national debt, indebtedness has also increased in other sectors of the economy: households, business and banking. Business debt is some 30% higher than normal in relation to GNP, while major banks are seriously exposed, partly through leveraged buyouts and third world loans.

International Indebtedness Over a period of a few years, the United States has ceased to be the world's largest creditor, and has become instead the world's largest debtor. The deficit on current account is running at around U.S. $120 billion per year, and the accumulated external debt is over U.S. $500 billion and rising steadily. The IMF expects that the current account deficit will worsen again next year, to around U.S. $140 billion; the dollar has weakened in the last few years and the U.S. internal deficit, coupled with the trade deficit, contributes to that process. The United States pays its "external debt" in U.S. dollars, which means essentially that it forces creditors to accept a currency that is steadily being weakened. This may be good for U.S. exports, but is damaging to holders of U.S. assets, as well as to countries that earn a large proportion of their foreign exchange receipts from exports of goods and services to the United States. Also, for the first time since 1958, the second quarter of 1988 showed a deficit on trade in services, reflecting the payments needed to service this international debt.

Of course, imbalances are a fact of international economic life. But the scale and rate of growth of the U.S. current account deficit is unprecedented. A substantial reorientation of the U.S. economy will be necessary to correct it, and, ultimately, to create a level of surplus needed to service the accumulated international obligations which could exceed U.S. $1 trillion.

The trade deficit is in fact a very serious problem. But it is important to recognize that it is itself a symptom of other problems. Its prime causes are a matter of heated debate. For some time, it was considered to be, primarily, the result of a strong dollar. However, after the Plaza agreement of 1986 between the U.S. and five of the world's leading economic powers and the dollar decline, its primary cause was considered to be an "unlevel playing field" of unfair practices by U.S. trading partners, particularly the Japanese. It is now increasingly recognized that the trade deficit is mainly the result of excess U.S. consumption financed by foreign borrowings, and of a decline in U.S. competitiveness.

Education, Social and Physical Infrastructure   There is a growing realization in the United States that the economic growth which made Americans feel good about themselves has been accompanied by the accumulation of serious social and physical problems. While the drug problem is in the forefront of public concern, there is a substantial agenda of problems postponed. Some of these, which will require attention and expenditure in due course are: improving education to meet the needs of a competitive economy; problems of urban poverty and growing racial tension; health care; a decaying physical infrastructure; and environmental problems, toxic and nuclear clean-up, etc.

The Security Trap   One of the main elements determining the balance of the U.S. budget is defence expenditure, at around U.S. $300 billion per year, or 7% of GNP. A substantial part of this expenditure serves to support the strategic objectives of the United States and its allies throughout the world. Now that the United States is facing economic difficulties, and competing head-on with countries whose security it guarantees, three major questions have arisen.

First, can the United States afford to devote such enormous financial and human resources to its own military security at a time when urgent economic and social problems threaten its future? Second, why should the United States continue to expend resources to improve the security of Western Europe and Japan (which spends only slightly more than 1% of GNP on defence) now that they are in a position to carry more substantial defence expenditures themselves? Third, the forty-year confrontation with the Soviet Union has virtually ended. Is this not an opportunity to reduce expenditures and use the resources to strengthen the competitive base of the U.S. economy and tackle accumulated social and environmental problems?

There are no easy answers to these questions. They demonstrate the degree to which economic and security issues are interlinked. A serious debate is now in progress, especially after the Gulf War, focused on the underlying question of what constitutes real security for the United States in the modern world. It is no longer simply a matter of military power: it must surely reflect the need to maintain the economic and technological strength of the country, its political influence in the world, and the health of its relations with its allies. In the longer term, global considerations of energy, environment, population and development are also components of real U.S. security.

Thus, the most powerful and wealthy economy in the world is confronting serious problems today, with the prospect of substantial and inescapable further demands on its resources in the future. In the absence of new policies, the deficits will remain high, and the accumulations of debt will increase. Such an evolution, through protectionism and trade war, volatility of exchange rates and loss of confidence, will threaten the world trade and monetary systems on which economic growth depends. It will become more and more difficult to generate discretionary resources, even for priority purposes such as the war on drugs, the improvement of education, or the stimulation of research, development and investment. Thus, the primary causes of the problems will remain unresolved.

Whatever proposals may be made for the international management of the world economy in the future, it is a prior condition that the budget and trade imbalances which confront the U.S. economy today must be corrected. Otherwise, these will be a constant source of instability and tension, and a threat to the world trade and monetary systems. They will also limit the effectiveness of the United States in world affairs at a time when its full participation will be badly needed.

THE JAPANESE ECONOMY

The most significant shift in the balance of world economic power in recent years has been the emergence of Japan as an economic superpower. The scale and speed of this change can be hard to appreciate. A few figures will make it clear. From 1985 to 1987, Japan's total national assets rose from U.S. $19.6 trillion to U.S. $43.7 trillion. During this same three-year period, the total national assets of the United

States climbed from U.S. $30.6 trillion to U.S. $36.2 trillion.

OECD estimates that the Japanese surplus will be U.S. $38 billion in 1990, $37 billion in 1991, and $36 billion in 1992. For comparison, the U.S. deficit is estimated to come down from U.S. $110 billion 1989 to $60 billion in 1992. The international assets of Japan may well reach U.S. $1 trillion in the mid-1990s. The Bank of Japan is now responsible for the world's largest reserves, of around U.S. $80 billion. As an actor in the world economic system, it is estimated that, between January 1986 and June 1987, the Bank of Japan spent U.S. $57 billion to press the decline of the dollar. Further, Japan is now the largest provider of development assistance, at U.S. $10 billion annually and is the second largest contributor to multilateral institutions such as the World Bank and the International Monetary Fund.

Japan has been providing a large part of the funds required every month to finance the U.S. budget deficit through the purchase of Treasury bonds at the rate of about U.S. $10 billion per month. In addition, Japanese corporations are investing in the United States—most recently, the purchase of Columbia Pictures Entertainment by Sony for U.S. $3.4 billion. In 1988 Japanese interests bought U.S. $16.5 billion of real estate, and nearly U.S. $13 billion in various companies. In all, Japan accounted for almost 19% of U.S. capital inflow in 1987.

The level of long-term interest rates has risen sharply in Japan, from 4.8% in 1988 to a forecast 7.9% in 1991 and 1992, while U.S. rates have remained broadly stable at around 8.7% and are now lower in real terms than in Japan. One reason is the determination of the Bank of Japan to wind back the wild inflation of asset prices which were supporting the expansion of bank lending.

Japan has consistently emphasized research and development, applied mainly to manufacturing in the civilian sector. The proportion of GNP applied to research and development has almost doubled in ten years, from 2% in 1980 to about 3.5% today. As an example of its vigorous technology, Japan introduces each year as many industrial robots as the rest of the world combined.

The political and economic system of Japan has twice demonstrated its ability to agree on new objectives and to reorient the whole economy in a very short time: first in response to the oil shock of 1973; more recently, in an effort to reduce its trade surpluses under the pressure of its trading partners, Japan has begun to reorient its economy so as to increase domestic consumption.

This ability to reach a consensus, and to achieve actual change in the orientation of the economy is an enormous asset for Japan in adapting to the increasing pace of change in the international economy. Financial institutions, corporations, unions, the education and research systems and the government itself all seem able to concert their efforts towards broad national goals. This capacity to adapt, coupled with the vast financial resources now available, a dynamic research and development system, and a high quality education system would seem to guarantee an even stronger economic surge in future years.

However, in spite of this tremendous strength, there are reasons for serious concern: the fragility of trading relations, the changing structure of the Japanese population, which by the year 2020 will count about 24% of the population over the age of sixty-five, but also a gradual shift in attitudes to work and new expectations for improvements in the conditions of daily life which is especially true of the younger generation. These trends will gradually affect the dynamics of the Japanese economy but they are unlikely to make a substantial change in its overall performance.

In the fields of money, trade, debt and development and in relations with its trading partners, Japan's traditional attitudes, policies and procedures will have to adapt to meet its new responsibilities as a major international power.

THE EUROPEAN COMMUNITY

In the early 1980s, while the economies of the United States and Japan enjoyed rapid expansion, it was fashionable to refer to "Eurosclerosis," which afflicted Europe with high unemployment and slow growth. In recent years, however, this situation has dramatically changed, for three main reasons.

First, increasing world trade, particularly resulting from U.S. economic expansion, has indeed provided a stimulus to European economies. Second, the domestic economic policies adopted in most European countries have helped to improve economic performance. And third, the decision to establish a unified European market, hopefully by 1993, has already provided a substantial economic and psychological boost across Europe.

It is now the Europeans who "feel good about themselves." They are engaged in a very rapid and far-reaching process of "European Perestroika" which would have seemed unthinkable only a few years ago.

How has this come about, and what are its implications? Perhaps the most important single cause was the feeling that unless Europe undertook some major initiative to improve its economic and technological performance, it was doomed to fall further behind not only the United States but also, and particularly, Japan.

Europe is now on the move towards a unified market of over 320 million inhabitants in which there will be relatively free movement of capital, labour, goods and services. This process is already underway, and most major corporations and banks are already positioning themselves to take advantage of the new situation through investments, mergers and takeovers. Also, there has been a surge of investment from countries outside the community, particularly Japan and the United States, so as to ensure that they are not subject to discrimination as outsiders to the Community.

This new surge of integration among the ancient nations of Europe is not simply an economic or technocratic matter. It is essentially a process of historic political significance. As the economic process proceeds, there will be important political decisions which will determine the future shape of the Community, of its institutions, and of its internal and external policies.

Many of the most difficult issues remain to be resolved and the final outcome is by no means clear.

The European Monetary Union has achieved a broad agreement among the twelve member countries on the first phase of the Delors plan to move towards monetary and economic union, and moved decisively forward at the Madrid Conference. Apart from the United Kingdom, at least provisionally, there is an agreement to work together to define a process for an eventual single currency.

The changes in Eastern Europe are so profound and so rapid that they cannot now be ignored in shaping the European Community after 1992. Among others, German reunification will transform in depth the nature of Europe and its role in the future. Whether the world economy will return to and maintain a higher rate of growth will depend to a considerable extent on the leadership, the policies, and the co-operation of the main economic powers, the European Community, Japan and the United States.

New patterns of co-operation should be developed to meet the global challenges of the next decades.

THE DEVELOPING COUNTRIES

From the point of view of the international management of the world economy, the term *developing countries* has little operational meaning. This broad grouping now covers such a wide range of countries that more precision is needed. It is more useful to analyse a number of key issues which will help clarify the functions required by the international system of the future.

Three such issues are outlined below: Debt; Poverty and Development; and Participation in the World Economy. Many other approaches are possible, but these issues do lead to insights into the future functions required.

The debt problem is no longer a threat to the international economic system given the provisions now made by the major banks and their reorientation away from lending to developing countries (in fact, the greatest risks for banks today are related to their domestic real estate lending). But debt remains a major domestic problem for many developing countries, especially in Latin America and Africa. In the last two years the Western Summit leaders have finally recognized that there is a problem of overindebtedness. First they have agreed to easier debt terms for poorer countries making efforts to improve their economic management (the so-called Toronto terms agreed on in 1988). Second, they have put in place a scheme to reduce the debt burdens for the larger debtors such as Mexico and Brazil (the Brady Plan). These are major steps forward, but they clearly need to be pursued with greater urgency and will need more resources than currently provided.

The growth of the world economy as a whole was nearly 4% in 1988, but that of Latin America was only six tenths of 1%. During that year, Latin American debt actually fell slightly, from U.S. $441 billion to U.S. $426 billion, as a result mainly of debt-to-equity conversion. But, over the twelve months to March 1989, the debt service burden grew by U.S. $10 billion, simply as a result of a 3% rise in international interest rates. The cost of debt service each year is a function of both interest rates and the value of the dollar, both evidently beyond the control of the countries concerned.

This dangerously unstable situation does not seem to elicit the urgent concern which it deserves. But the problem, if unattended, may well undermine the prospects for the world economy for several reasons. First, a number of major U.S. banks, although they have reduced their exposure, are still carrying substantial amounts of developing country loans in relation to their capital.

Second, since 1984, the developing countries have been transferring money to the developed countries, a "net negative transfer" of repayments in excess of new lending. The amount of this transfer was over U.S. $50 billion in 1988. Compounding this problem, the total flow of direct foreign investment to developing countries has fallen from U.S. $25 billion in 1982 to U.S. $13 billion in 1987.

Thus, at a time when the developing countries urgently need resources, there is a substantial net flow from poor to rich countries. And, in effect, the developed debtor countries, particularly the United States, are competing for resources with the poor countries of the developing world. This is inequitable, and represents a tremendous waste of human and economic potential. Indeed, the abrupt decline of the economies of Latin America alone resulted in a substantial loss of U.S. exports and employment.

On its own, the indebtedness of the developing countries would constitute a serious and growing threat to world economic and political stability. But the debt problem must be seen in the context of the other serious trade and financial imbalances among the developed countries. In this perspective, the international management of the world economy seems very inadequate. And the hopeful and reassuring prospects of steady economic growth seem doubtful.

New resources will also be needed on a substantial scale to stimulate development at a time when there are new competing claims, for example in Eastern Europe and from the countries directly affected by the Gulf crisis. It is also essential that the access of the debtor countries to the markets of the North be maintained and expanded. If protectionism increases in the North, this will greatly aggravate the debt problem, as it has in the past. To develop a viable approach to the debt and development problem will require a far more coherent linkage of policies and institutions concerned with financial management (IMF), with investment and development (the World Bank), and trade (UNCTAD, GATT).[2] This will be a central challenge to the world community demanding above all imaginative, co-operative efforts by the United States, Europe and Japan. In spite of institutional reluctance, policy objectives and action in such interlinked fields as finance, debt management, investment, development, policy, human resource development, trade and environment must be made more coherent.

Another issue, even more threatening to the world in the long term than debt, is that of population growth, poverty and a decline in the level of development in many countries of the South such as Bangla Desh, Burkina Faso and Haiti.

Perhaps inevitably, the interest of politicians, business leaders, intellectuals and the public in the developed countries is focused on issues that immediately affect their welfare. Thus, the prospects for increased world economic growth provide reassurance in the short term. The long-term implications of the present

---

[2]United Nations Commission for Trade and Development, General Agreement on Tariffs and Trade.

path of the world economy—increasingly divided and polarized between a small percentage of the rich (perhaps 20% in 2025) and a vast percentage of the poor and frustrated—seem far away. But they are not. Apart from ethical considerations, which seem to have a very limited motivational force, two practical implications are likely to become painfully evident relatively soon.

In a number of poor countries, governments will begin to respond to the intense pressures of their youthful, frustrated populations, increasingly concentrated in vast cities. There is no reason to expect that they will act in accordance with the norms of behaviour established predominantly by Westerners in laying the foundations of the international system forty years ago. After decades of United Nations resolutions, North–South dialogues and conferences, with little positive result, they may well move towards confrontation. That this may be illogical or costly would be irrelevant to the political realities at work. History offers many parallels for this evolution.

Under such conditions, the comfortable assumptions of international affairs would no longer apply. At the least, the delicate network of international travel, of health and security controls, of diplomatic courtesies, business and scientific contacts, etc. would all be threatened. At the worst, terrorism and conflict —with its ensuing migration flows—would drastically increase, which would certainly attract the attention of the North.

The pressures of a rapidly growing population on the world environment are already becoming all too evident. But the solution cannot be found in the environmental area alone. Generally, the causes of environmental problems are a complex mixture of human needs, economic pressures, technological options and political interests. Knowledge, resources, sensitivity and commitment are needed to resolve them. There is now wide public awareness that Planet Earth is one delicate system: the destruction of the environment in the South threatens the North, and vice versa. In the environmental area, there are now the preconditions for international action.

Participation in the World Economy The outline of the developed economies presented above demonstrates the enormous potential of new technologies, management practices and public policies to promote a new surge of growth. But at the same time, the demand of these powerful economies for the products of the developing countries is likely to diminish as a result of technological progress, automation, and their changing demographic structure. The shift from natural to synthetic products and new materials has continued, moreover, to weaken the markets for most basic products which still are the main source of export proceeds for most developing countries.

A number of developing countries, such as South Korea, Singapore or Malaysia, Brazil, and more recently Mexico, which are able to compete successfully, attract investment and generate a modern economic base, may effectively become full participants in the developed part of the world economy. In other countries, the modern part of a dual economy may develop strong links to the northern economies, unconnected to the rest of the country. In any event, most developing countries stand in need of access to modern technology and of enhanced scientific and technological co-operation.

For many poorer countries, and for the poorer parts of dual economies, the economic opportunities will be limited. Demand for their primary products from the North is unlikely to increase significantly; they are unlikely to be able to develop a significant manufacturing base; the advantage of cheap labour will diminish as automation in the North reduces labour content; and the potential of the "knowledge revolution," of information and computer technology, telecommunications, etc., is likely to prove a mirage. This is because the trained and educated manpower, the systems and the infrastructure on which it must be based are lacking.

Another critical aspect will be the growing competition for resources of all kinds—particularly energy, water and viable land for living—as world population grows and environmental problems increase. The orderly distribution of such resources through the market price mechanism, or by government allocation, will come under increasing pressure as demands become more desperate. This issue will require urgent attention at the international level. It will be one of the necessary functions of the future, on both practical and ethical grounds.

In the absence of a significant new strategy for world development, the world economy is likely to become even more polarized and divided between the rich and the poor. Already today, about 1.3 billion people, more than 20% of world population are seriously sick or malnourished, according to the World Health Organisation.

In this perspective it is alarming to note that the

aid performance of the developed countries may be deteriorating. Since 1970 their aid provision has expanded broadly in line with their economic growth (i.e., at about 3% per annum). While year to year the aid growth fluctuates, the average for the past four years has been less than 2%. In 1989 the amount was U.S. $46.7, about 0.33% of the GNP of the developed countries, down from an average of 0.35% for the last 20 years (the UN target is set at 0.75%). Within this average, some countries have consistently maintained an aid level of around 1%, while others remain well below the average. An increase in ODA (Official Development Aid) is particularly important to the poorest countries: they have very limited options available to promote their development.

The improvement in relations between East and West now creates the possibility of a truly global effort. Also, over $1 trillion U.S. dollars is now spent worldwide on armaments each year, including U.S. $200 billion by developing countries. Therefore, substantial human and investment resources could gradually be released for development through the reduction of arms expenditures throughout the world.

New thinking is badly needed: to ignore the issue will lead to disaster. And simply to promote "growth" throughout the developing world along the lines followed by the Western economies is not a viable strategy on environmental and other grounds. This cannot be an excuse for stagnation: it is a reason for new approaches to development.

THE SOVIET UNION AND EASTERN EUROPE

Until quite recently, the Soviet Union and the countries of Eastern Europe did not play a substantial role in the world economy. Now the situation is rapidly changing and they will become a factor of increasing importance for the following main reasons:

The success of Perestroika in the Soviet Union, and of those Eastern European countries engaged in reform, depends to a certain extent on trade and technological co-operation with the West. As reform continues, the intensity of such co-operation will increase, and this will be of particular importance to Western Europe, especially to the Federal Republic of Germany. Reflecting this, the leaders of the seven Western industrial countries, meeting in Paris in July 1990, assigned a co-ordinating role to the European Commission in this area.

The Soviet Union and the Eastern European countries, particularly Poland, are facing enormous budgetary and financial difficulties. The budget deficit of the Soviet Union for 1988 amounted to 120 billion rubles, or about U.S. $190 billion at the official rate. For 1990, it is planned to reduce this to 60 billion rubles, about U.S. $94 billion. There is a vast accumulation of problems to be solved, and the benefits anticipated from Perestroika have not yet begun to appear. From the consumer's point of view, the situation is in fact worse than before.

In these circumstances, finance and investment from the West is of great importance. Although it has entered into loan agreements, particularly with German banks, the Soviet Union seems reluctant to take up the credit now available. Poland, however, is urgently seeking resources for immediate use. Two important issues arise: First, until economic management improves, will additional financial resources from the West be effectively utilized? Second, until it is clear that reform will succeed, and that a reformed Soviet Union will not revert to its past policy of confrontation with the West, should the West provide support?

This second question is proving divisive in the West. Western European countries emphasize the opportunity and the need to encourage positive change, while some elements in the United States emphasize the risk, and the need for caution. If the Soviet Union should decide to move much faster, even incurring substantial debt to accelerate economic results through co-operation with the West, this problem will become acute.

Relations with Japan   One of the certainties of international relations since the Second World War has been that relations between the Soviet Union and Japan would not significantly improve, for two reasons. First, the warm and intense relationship of Japan with the United States precluded good relations with the Soviet Union, at least during the period of East–West tensions. Second, the vehement disagreement between Japan and the Soviet Union over the Kurile Islands prevented any rapprochement.

Looking into the future, both of these considerations may change. At a time of reduced East–West tensions and because of an increasingly difficult relationship with the United States, Japan may feel more inclined to improve its relations with the Soviet Union. And, the Soviet Union may wish to strengthen its ties to Japan in order to benefit from its financial and technological resources. Such an evolution would have major repercussions for the structure of the world economy, and for international relations in general.

Beyond these rather specific instances, there is one aspect of overriding importance where the policies and prospects of the Soviet Union and its allies are of immense importance to the future of the world. For more than forty years, the rivalry and tension between East and West have perverted international relations and obstructed growth and progress throughout the world. It now appears that, as long as President Gorbachev remains in power, relations between East and West are set on a new, constructive course.

Whether this situation is already irreversible, or whether the failure of Perestroika to fulfill expectations would result in a return to confrontation is beyond the scope of this paper. But one conclusion is inescapable. Every effort must be made to consolidate the progress which has already been made away from East–West confrontation, and towards a reduction in armaments. This will have positive repercussions throughout the world, for two reasons.

First, and most evident, it will help to reduce tensions and thus the resources devoted to armaments. These resources can then become available for investment, and for the provision of the desperately needed social services. Second, the reduction of tensions, conflict and threat will have an important moral and psychological effect. This should not be underestimated. It could create the conditions for constructive new initiatives in which East and West could co-operate for the first time, mobilizing their energies to face global problems. This is perhaps the greatest single opportunity available at the present time to consolidate the progress which has been made and to open new ways for future global co-operation.

IV

INTIMATIONS
OF SOLIDARITY

IN A DECLARATION MADE BY THE CLUB OF
Rome in 1985 we said, "there could be a bright and
fulfilling future awaiting humanity if it has the wisdom to reach out and grasp the difficulties ahead, or a
slow and painful decline if it neglects to do so." This
is still our credo, but time has grown short.

In the previous chapters we have outlined some of
the negative and dangerous trends in contemporary
society, but there are many positive aspects which
give hope that humanity is aware of its problems and
that the race has the urge, the creativity and the
adaptability to face its future.

In this chapter we shall mention a few of these
signs of hope as an encouragement to the reader.

For the last forty-five years, ideological polariza-
tion between the two superpowers has held the world
in a state of hypnosis and of apprehension of nuclear
disaster. Erosion of the influence of the superpowers

> "There are three possibilities facing mankind. The first is that it will initiate nuclear war, after which there will be nothing to worry about. The second is that it will be willing to take a thousand small, wise decisions and pull gradually out of the mess. The third and most probable is that it will do nothing and that the situation will deteriorate so that the poor will inherit the earth and live in misery for ever after."
>
> Paraphrased from Harrison Brown*

and now the sudden collapse of the centrally planned economies has neutralized the tensions, presenting us with an entirely new *mise en scène*. Agreements on arms reduction already accomplished and the expectation of much more to come is an achievement far beyond anything that could have been imagined a decade ago. This opens the way to more serious attention to the other problems which, in their conjunction, make up the "predicament of mankind."[1]

The new spirit of co-operation between the United States and the Soviet Union has made possible a high degree of solidarity between the nations against aggression, as evidenced by the action of the UN Security Council and General Assembly to agree on a world blockade of Iraq following its occupation of Kuwait in 1990.

---

* Personal communication, 1978 (Harrison Brown was at that time Professor at California Institute of Technology)
[1] "The Predicament of Mankind" was the name of the original research project of the Club of Rome at its very beginning.

After lengthy negotiations, the Law of the Seas Conference agreed on many important actions and novel institutional measures. It endorsed the concept of the oceans as the "common heritage of mankind." This precedent has also been applied to Antarctica, the last and extremely fragile unexploited area of the planet, which otherwise would have been pillaged by the greedy industrial nations in search of new resources, leading to ecological disaster.

There has been in recent years an encouragingly great increase of public awareness of the dangers which face us, due initially to the analyses of groups such as the Club of Rome and promoted by the media. Worldwide public debate, the pressure of green lobbies, events such as the Chernobyl and Bhopal disasters have forced politicians to recognize the potential importance of a whole series of new issues and industry to adopt at least the appearance of social and environmental responsibility.

As a consequence of awakened public awareness, new signs of responsibility and solidarity have appeared and are spreading, in the form of citizens groups, co-operatives and NGOs with a vast variety of aims and methods, concerned with local national and world problems.

Particularly impressive has been the response of many private and volunteer agencies to disaster situations in places remote from their bases. This has been outstanding in a number of earthquake relief operations. During the acute situations of famine in Ethiopia and the Sahel, NGOs appear to have been more effective than governments and the international agencies in bringing food rapidly to the starving. In general, nongovernmental activity has achieved a new order of magnitude and importance and bids fair to have a growing and constructive influence on national and international policies.

Despite the relative failure of development and aid policies, some countries have achieved spectacular successes. India, one of the most populous countries, has become a major industrial power in addition to its agricultural achievements through the green revolution. The Asian Dragons, otherwise known as the NICs (the newly industrialized countries of South East Asia—Taiwan, Singapore, Hong Kong and South Korea) have created great prosperity based to a large extent on exploitation of the new technologies. There is a lesson here for other struggling nations. The Dragons, following the example of Japan, founded their development on the generalization and upgrading of education and the creation of sound scientific infrastructures. Some of the poorer countries are also showing the results of creative initiative, for example recent progress in Botswana and consistent development in Zimbabwe.

A significant event has been the exercise of "people's power," supported by world public opinion, leading to the downfall of oppressive governments in Eastern Europe. These are manifestations which, ten years earlier, would have been suppressed by military intervention. This type of bloodless revolution is a rare event in world history and contrasts with the brutal crushing of popular will a few months earlier in China and to the tragic events in Rumania. Changes in Chile have been positive and there is a trend to democracy in many other places. The recent volte-face in Ethiopia is unexpected and hopes arise now for settlements in Central America and even for the disappearance of apartheid in South Africa, despite the danger of civil war in that country. In many African countries which have been ruled by dictators and single party politics since independence, public unrest is beginning to win concessions. Thus, as we come to the last decade of this millennium, we find democracy has emerged as the triumphant and preferred ideology of the whole world, while dictatorial ideologies both of the left and of the right have fallen into disrepute. One can only hope this will be irreversible.

A new kind of relationship between heads of state and ministers has begun to emerge. Through numerous multilateral or bilateral conferences, meetings and telephone calls, personal relations are being established which enable a better understanding among the human beings behind the official functions. This is creating a new network of rapid communication at the highest level, even if it does not always lead to common action.

Enormous benefits have flowed from advances in medical sciences and in the spreading of improved hygiene. In the North, the scourge of tuberculosis, despite local flare-ups, has almost gone; life expectancy has increased and cures or alleviations found for many illnesses. Smallpox has been eliminated by a well-planned international effort and hopes exist for the conquest of several other diseases which plague the tropical countries. Perhaps even more important has been the significant reduction of infant mortality in the developing countries, partly through improved hygiene, greatly through the introduction of a simple method of curing infantile diarrhea and more recently by immunization against measles, that major killer of children in tropical and equatorial climates. All in all, "death control" has been more successful than birth control in the developing world.

World recognition of the importance of human rights has been a positive feature in recent years and should continue to be so. Bodies such as Amnesty International have been successful in exposing abuses everywhere and without political bias. Nevertheless the fashionable appeal to human rights has served as a manipulative alibi to cover up unseemly practices in many countries. Here we must stress the conviction of the Club that the maintenance of human rights must be complemented by an equivalent acceptance of human responsibility. This applies at the individual, national and international levels.

A promising and prompt approach to a solution of a global problem by international action has been the (at present partial) agreement for the elimination of the CFCs to which we have already referred.

We have also mentioned the trend to end dangerous, dirty and boringly repetitive work in industry as a consequence of robotization. Also, interesting attempts are being made to replace line assembly by new methods of group working which give the members of the team a variety of tasks to do and allow for individual involvement which makes it possible to have pride in work and craftsmanship.

This century has witnessed great advances in the position of women in the Western countries, first in gaining the franchise of the vote, later being accepted in employment outside the family and now edging towards equal pay for equal work with men. In many cultures women have been exploited by men, restricted to the family and given a secondary place in society. Of course intelligent women have, throughout the ages, exerted great influence through their men, but that is no longer sufficient. Today women work side by side with men, sit in parliament, become business leaders and prime ministers, although still in rather modest numbers in the higher posts. This is good, but still not enough. The aggressive feminism of the 1970s and 1980s somehow missed the point. In demanding an artificial equality with men, rather than one which is essentially complementary, women found they had no other choice but to reproduce the sterile male logic which has led the world into its present state of malaise. In the process many of the most successful became, as it were, male-hearted women, instead of developing the virtues of the female mind which society so badly needs.

This phase happily seems to be passing. There is increasing recognition among both men and women of the significance of female qualities and values. Women are at last accepting that they can and must behave as women rather than attempt to beat men at their own games. Equally men, and the managerial, economic and political systems they have created, are beginning to recognize the importance of women's skills as managers of both people and resources, as communicators and, above all that their versatility is vital for the development of a healthy and balanced society. This recognition by both sexes is a crucially important step forward and the opportunity to enable and encourage women to contribute fully to the running of society must not be wasted. The battle is not yet fully won. Much male chauvinism persists, but it will pass with the generations.

Two elements are paramount if women are to be

enabled to contribute actively and constructively to social development. First, society must both listen to and place confidence in women. In the male dominated and seemingly rational world of today, female intuition, versatility and innate common sense are too often ignored—often at a heavy cost.

Second, women will have to be given support from society, both financial and moral. Such support needs to be flexible and sensitive to allow women to play a positive role in the shaping of society, without compromising their place at the heart of the family. In the West, this means flexible work patterns, comprehensive child care and equal opportunities. In the developing world this means extensive legal rights as well as political and financial support. In some countries, availability of credit to women for the first time has unleashed a wealth of initiative and creative activity.

But above all women must listen to themselves and support each other. They must develop confidence in their abilities and stop an inexplicable tendency to denigrate themselves in judging themselves against male criteria.

So we can see that the seeds of mutual responsibility are cast. We have to call for an enlarged jointly responsible action.

V

THE VACUUM

ORDER IN SOCIETY IS DETERMINED BY THE cohesion of its members. Until the middle of our century, this was normally ensured by a natural patriotism, a sense of belonging to the community, reinforced by a moral discipline exerted by religion and respect for the state and its leaders, however remote they might be from the people. Meanwhile, generalized religious faith has evaporated in many countries; respect for the political process has also faded, owing partly to the media, leading to indifference if not hostility, and partly to the inadequacy of the political parties in facing real problems; minorities are less and less willing to respect the decisions of the majority. Thus a vacuum has been created, in which both order and objectives in society are being corroded.

Today's approach is superficial. It is based on current events and dangers as they are perceived and on crisis government attempts to eliminate symptoms of causes that have not been diagnosed. This is the way we are setting the scene for mankind's encounter with the planet.

We look in vain for wisdom. The opposition between the two ideologies that have dominated the century has collapsed, forming their own vacuum and leaving nothing but crass materialism. Nothing within the governmental system and its decision-making process seems capable of opposing or modifying these trends which raise questions about our common future and indeed about the very survival of the race.

We must ask whether these are signs of an individual and collective resignation in face of the vastness of the task facing humanity and the urgent need for action; or is this a sign of lack of imagination and incapacity to invent new ways and new means which will measure up to the globalization of the problems? The task is indeed formidable, but if we show no sign of accepting its challenge, the people may well panic, lose faith in their leaders, give in to fear and offer support to those extremists who know well how to turn popular fear to their own advantage with incendiary charismatic speeches.

It is a law of Nature that any vacuum will be filled and therefore eliminated unless this is physically prevented. "Nature," as the saying goes, "abhors a vacuum." And people, as children of Nature, can only feel uncomfortable, even though they may not recognize that they are living in a vacuum. How then is the vacuum to be eliminated? Like the black holes of space which suck in everything that approaches, the vacuum of society seems to attract the best and the worst at random. We can but hope that the semi-chaos which is now taking over will eventually provide the material for a self-organised system with new possibilities. The system is not yet hopeless, but human wisdom must be marshalled quickly if we are to survive.

"How simple things were with Brezhnev," a European leader confided, half seriously and half ironically. The collapse of communism in the Eastern European countries and the Soviet Union constitutes a major and unsettling factor in this coming turn of the century. The new hands that are to be dealt in the card game of politics are unlikely to be assessed at their true value or their potential consequences evaluated until at least two or three decades have gone by.

The implosion of the ideology that dominated the greater part of the twentieth century was certainly spectacular, but was by no means the only one. It coincides with the end of the "American dream," which lost its credibility with the painful Vietnam War that deeply scarred the collective conscience, with the failure of Challenger, Hispanic migration, poverty within plenty, drugs, violence and AIDS and the fact that the "melting pot" no longer works. Having lost its position of unique leadership in the world —a leadership compounded of a generosity laced with Puritan values and a cynicism worthy of the conquerors of the Far West—the American nation is plunged into doubt and facing the temptation, so often resisted and no longer possible in the global village, of withdrawing into itself.

Most of the poor countries are gradually relinquishing Marxist and socialist incantations in favour of more concrete and immediate preoccupations such as economic development and the stabilization of their economies. Capitalist and free-market economies have found it necessary to make adjustments for them to survive socially, while socialist systems also made adjustments belatedly, but did not survive. Only materialism remains today a strong all-pervading countervalue. The grand political and economic theories which motivated the action of some and aroused the opposition of others appear to have run their course.

It is not easy to stimulate universal debate on ideas, but the lack of attempts to do so still further deepens the vacuum. There is pressing need for such a debate, and the multitudinous occasions for international encounters, with their cross-cultural discussions, should initiate new and more global thinking.

This period of absence of thought and of lack of a common vision—not of what the world of tomorrow will be, but of what we want it to be so that we can shape it—is one source of discouragement and even despair. How simple it was, or should have been, for France, Great Britain and their allies to mobilize against their common Nazi enemy. And was it not obvious during the period of the cold war that the Western nations should accomplish a diplomatic, economic and technological mobilization against the Soviet Union and the satellite countries? Again, freedom fighters, despite tribal and ideological differences, were able to find unity and strengthened patriotism in the struggle for independence from the common enemy, the Colonial power. It would seem that men and women need a common motivation, namely a common adversary to organise and act together; in the vacuum such motivations seem to have ceased to exist—or have yet to be found.

The need for enemies seems to be a common historical factor. States have striven to overcome domestic failure and internal contradictions by designating external enemies. The scapegoat practice is as old as mankind itself. When things become too difficult at home, divert attention by adventure abroad. Bring the divided nation together to face an outside enemy, either a real one or else one invented for the purpose. With the disappearance of the traditional enemy, the temptation is to designate as scapegoat religious or ethnic minorities whose differences are disturbing.

Can we live without enemies? Every state has been so used to classifying its neighbours as friend or foe that the sudden absence of traditional adversaries has left governments and public opinion with a great void. New enemies, therefore, have to be identified, new strategies imagined, new weapons devised. The new enemies may have changed in nature and location, but they are no less real. They threaten the whole human race and their names are pollution, water shortage, famine, malnutrition, illiteracy, unemployment. However, it appears that awareness of the new enemies is, as yet, insufficient to elicit world cohesion and solidarity for the fight. Also the collapse of the ideologies has removed some of the necessary points of reference.

Two axes of reference have made possible political evolution that has shaken the world these last years and led to the downfall of many dictatorships. These are human rights and democracy. We shall analyse their strengths and limitations.

The concept of human rights has been, during the

past decade, a factor of mobilization that became effective through its dissemination by the media and by word of mouth in the countries where those rights were disregarded and denied. When freedom was widely enjoyed in other countries, how could the people be deprived of it indefinitely? This is especially the case in countries such as Poland or Brazil where the Catholic Church, an ardent protagonist and supporter of human rights, was strong.

In some of the most totalitarian of countries, aspirations of freedom have been achieved as if the pressure of values had reached a yield point and the lid suddenly blew off the pot. Through various processes and with the painful cost of civil struggle, death and imprisonment, this thirst for freedom was expressed around men as different as Martin Luther King, Lech Walesa, Vaclav Havel, Don Helder Camara or Nelson Mandela, just as in earlier years Mahatma Gandhi had paved the way.

But freedom alone cannot reorganise a state, write a constitution, create a market and economic growth, rebuild industry and agriculture or build a new social structure. It is a necessary and noble inspiration, but is far from being an operating manual for a new government. This is why the concept of human rights simply initiates but cannot implement the process of democratization.

This is where the question must be raised—what democracy and for what purposes?

The old democracies have functioned reasonably well over the last two hundred years, but they appear now to be in a phase of complacent stagnation with little evidence of real leadership and innovation. It is to be hoped, with the newfound enthusiasm for democracy in the liberated countries today, that people will not reproduce slavish copies of existing models that are unable to meet contemporary needs.

THE LIMITS OF DEMOCRACY

Democracy is not a panacea. It cannot organise everything and it is unaware of its own limits. These facts must be faced squarely, sacrilegious though this may sound. As now practiced, democracy is no longer well suited for the tasks ahead. The complexity and the technical nature of many of today's problems do not always allow elected representatives to make competent decisions at the right time. Few politicians in office are sufficiently aware of the global nature of the problems in front of them and have little if any awareness of the interactions between the problems. Generally speaking, informed discussion on the main political, economic and social issues takes place on radio and television rather than in Parliament to the detriment of the latter. Political party activities are so intensely focused on election deadlines and party rivalries that they end up weakening the democracy they are supposed to serve. This confrontational approach gives an impression that party needs come before national interest. Strategies and tactics seem more important than do objectives and often a constituency is neglected as soon as it is conquered. With the current mode of operation, Western democracies are seeing their formal role decline and public opinion drifting away from elected representatives. However, the crisis in the contemporary democratic system must not be allowed to serve as an excuse for rejecting democracy as such.

In the countries now opening up to freedom, democracy is being introduced in a situation which demands of the citizens greatly changed attitudes and patterns of behaviour. The inevitable problems of phasing in democracy are difficult. But there is another, still more serious question. Democracy does not necessarily build the bridge between a colonial or neocolonial economy, or a centralized bureaucratic economy towards a market economy based on competition and producing growth. In a transitional situation such as the present, which, because of sudden and unforeseen change, has been neither planned nor prepared for, the necessary structures, attitudes, market relations and managerial styles simply do not exist. If such a situation is allowed to go on too long, it is probable that democracy will be made to seem responsible for the lagging economy, the scarcities and uncertainties. The very concept of democracy could then be brought into question and allow for the seizure of power by extremists of one brand or the other.

Winston Churchill was right when he quipped, "Democracy is the worst of all systems, except for the rest." Yet we must be aware of its erosion, its fragility and its limitations. When persons say that "the things that have to be done to improve our situation are perfectly obvious," they seldom ask "Why aren't they done then?" And if they do, they answer, "because we lack the (political) will or because of habits, or shortsightedness, or politics, etc., etc." Our inability to indicate how to overcome these sources of inertia and resistance makes it clear that what should be done is not obvious at all. We overlook (psychologically speaking, we deny) our ignorance and instead say, "All we lack is the political will."

The crucial need is to revitalize democracy and give it a breadth of perspective that will enable it to cope with the evolving global situation. In other words, is this new world we find ourselves in governable? The answer is: probably not with the existing structures and attitudes. Have we gathered the necessary means and wisdom to make decisions on the scale of the world problematique, taking into account the exigencies of time? There is an increasingly evident contradiction between the urgency of making some decisions and the democratic procedure founded on various dialogues such as parliamentary debate, public debate and negotiations with trade unions or professional organisations. The obvious advantage of this procedure is its achievement of consensus; its disadvantage lies in the time it takes, especially at the international level. For indeed the difficulty is not only in the making of decisions, but also in their implementation and evaluation. Time in these matters has acquired a deep ethical content. The costs of delay are monstrous in terms of human life and hardship as well as of resources. The slowness of decision in a democratic system is particularly damaging at the international level. When dictators attack and international policing is required, delays of decisions can be fatal.

The problem then is to invent instruments of governance capable of mastering change without violence and of maintaining a quality of peace which encourages rather than inhibits a state of security, fairness and fulfilling growth for individuals and societies alike. Not only have we to find better means of governance at national and international levels, but we have also to determine the characteristics of a capacity to govern. Global "governance," in our vocabulary, does not imply a global "government," but rather the institutions of co-operation, co-ordination and common action between durable sovereign states. The good, and for our purposes, encouraging news is that:

- people and nations are beginning to agree to take "next steps" together (however, they are carefully avoiding to agree on *why* they are agreeing);

- this seems to be happening by practical consensus procedures rather than by the formal voting of instructed governmental representatives;

- many international functions, especially those requiring the most foresight and operational flexibility, can be carried out through non-governmental arrangements;

- in many fields governments have already come to realize that effective deployment of their most cherished right, their sovereignty, requires that it be *pooled* with the sovereignty of other nations, in order to do things that none of them can do alone. In this sense, co-operation does not mean relinquishing sovereignty, but rather exerting it through joint action, instead of losing it or just not using it.

Whether on the international scale, at the national level or that of the corporation, the problem of governance presents itself in new terms.

The growing complexity of the world and of its problems makes it necessary to have a complete grasp on tremendous amounts of information before coming to a decision. This immediately calls to account the quality of information, for it is under constant danger of rapid obsolescence, possible inaccuracy or outright propaganda.

A second impediment to governance is caused by the increasing size and inertia of large bureaucracies that spread their tentacles around the centres of power and slow down or paralyze both decision making and implementation. Other crucial impediments consist of the lack of education for competent citizenship and inadequate intergenerational understanding.

Yet another difficulty arises from the importance of economy within the administration and its sectoral structures. If the different power centres do not learn to co-operate and instead insist on acting in ignorance or in opposition to one another, the resulting administrative sluggishness can provoke delays that can lead to inefficiency, wrong decisions and confrontation. So far, governance has operated by treating problems separately and in a vertical mode. Today the interaction between problems is such that no single issue can even be approached, to say nothing of resolved, outside of the framework of the problematique.

This in turn demands leaders of a new kind, capable of treating problems both horizontally and vertically. In the world that is emerging, decision making can no longer be the monopoly of governments and their departments, working in, yes, a vacuum. There is need to bring many partners into the process— business and industry, research institutions, scientists, NGOs and private organisations—so that the widest available experience and skill is available.

And, of course, an enlightened public support, aware of the new needs and of the possible consequences would be essential. A dynamic world needs an effective nervous system at the grass-roots level, not only to ensure the widest range of inputs, but to make possible the identification of all citizens with the common process of governance.

In the present, vacuous situation, lack of identification of people with the processes of society is expressed as indifference, skepticism or outright rejection of governments and political parties, seen as having little control over the problems of our times. These attitudes are indicated by a decreasing rate of participation in elections.

The Common Enemy of Humanity Is Man

In searching for a new enemy to unite us, we came up with the idea that pollution, the threat of global warming, water shortages, famine and the like would fit the bill. In their totality and in their interactions these phenomena do constitute a common threat which demands the solidarity of all peoples. But in designating them as the enemy, we fall into the trap about which we have already warned, namely mistaking symptoms for causes. All these dangers are caused by human intervention and it is only through changed attitudes and behaviour that they can be overcome. The real enemy, then, is humanity itself.

VI

THE HUMAN
MALAISE

THE SHOCK WAVES PRODUCED BY THE DRAS-
tic changes of the great transition are sparing no region, no society. The upheaval has broken up a
system of relationships and belief systems inherited
from the past without giving any guidelines for the
future.

There are so many reasons for doubts and despair:
the disappearance of values and references; the increasing complexity and uncertainty of the world
and the difficulty of understanding the new emerging
global society; unsolved problems such as continuing
environmental deterioration and extreme poverty
and underdevelopment in the southern countries; the
impact of mass media often operating as a magnifying
glass for a crushing reality and a throbbing song of
calamity.

Let us mention, without attempting an in-depth
analysis, a list of various symptoms. Although different from each other in their nature and their conse-

quences, all share the quality of being worldwide symptoms: the waves of violence, particularly in big cities, the permanence of international terrorism, the acts of national mafias that are also rapidly becoming international networks; the rise of drug addiction and drug-related crime; the aggressive exhibitionism in sexuality and deviant behaviour exploited by the press, mass media and advertising worlds.

All of these circumstances are setting the stage, on many different levels, for a new and upsetting environment, where marginal behaviour in general is given so much and such repeated coverage that it is being perceived as commonplace.

Parents and teachers, the reference point of most societies, have not been prepared by their education to adjust to the new situation imposed upon them today. As the late American sociologist Margaret Mead remarked: "Young people are the native population of this new world in which we adults are immigrants." Some of us would even go along with her observation that "nowhere in the world do there exist adults who know what their children know, however remote or simple the societies in which those children live. In the past, there were always some elders who knew more—had more experience or practice of a system in which they had grown up—than any child. Today there are no longer any."

Everywhere, teachers are facing difficulties with their pupils and students for they too are unprepared for teaching young people who are much more independent than they were at the same age, and considerably better informed and misinformed through the mass media. All sorts of institutions, such as the political parties or trade unions, are discovering how difficult it is to relate to their constituencies in the old-fashioned way. This crisis of relationships is a crisis of dialogue. And absence of dialogue leads to confrontation.

This does not simply mean that parents and teachers have ceased to be guides; it means that there are no longer any guides in the old sense of the term, whether one looks for them in one's own country, in China, in India, in Africa, in America or in Europe.

Thanks to modern means of information, young people are being rapidly exposed to more and more facts that give them reason to consider their elders as lacking responsibility and awareness with regard to enormous dangers such as nuclear holocaust, pollution and the violent destruction of environment. Furthermore, a shower of unrelated disasters and news reports on everyday violence are like a series of shocks that lead to the feeling of generalized disorder.

Within this changed pattern, what happens to the life of the individual? Children watch television and learn about all aspects of human life. They learn to be persons with individual choices, inclinations and freedoms. Antagonism between inherited and acquired values is such that if a young person wants to think and act for himself, he must have lots of courage or he will break down.

Not having been given the means to discern what is fundamental in traditions and values, and what is merely their formal expression, the younger generation is rejecting traditions and values as a whole and is sketching out new trends: today, adolescents are the ones who know about and contribute to the major transnational currents and try to stand firm against the dangers. Their parents now have to seek their consent and negotiate their own formerly unquestioned authority.

How do parents and teachers react to this reversal, where the exercise of authority is disrupted and the "master" no longer acknowledged? Some, still adolescent or emotionally immature, adopt the young people's fads of the moment and imitate the way they dress and speak. Those who lose all authority over their children are usually themselves unsure of their own identity and values, and transmit their own malaise to the young.

For these disturbed parents of disturbed young people, there is only one way out, which is not to mime but to truly listen to and learn from their children, even if the theories the children profess seem at first to them unacceptable, unworkable or impossible to put into practice. There is a need, now more than ever, to establish a fruitful intergenerational dialogue.

In almost all cultures, the family cell is regarded as a fundamental value. It will probably continue as such, but in new circumstances—a family disjointed and shattered by urban life, rural exodus, emigration and conflicts; modified by our control over reproduction, with the human couple now joined in an uncertain bond; functioning according to a new pattern of relationships that has replaced the hitherto uncontested parental authority; a family within which the upholders of tradition are increasingly in conflict with those of an American-style modernity.

"In India," explains Mrs. Parthaswarathi, the Principal of a girls' school in New Delhi, "the crisis has already arrived. The young are living a perilous existence, torn between the traditional and the new values and subjected to contradictory pressures. They must continually make up their minds and take decisions in a context where the family used to decide collectively, with the last word belonging to the patriarch."

"Indeed, man is in distress! Except for those who believe and do good deeds, and command the law among themselves and command patient endurance among themselves."

Koran: Verse 103

The present malaise is affecting societies and individuals lost in their brutal break with the past with no new, coherent vision of the future to go by. Who am I, where am I going, why? Although these are the eternal, traditional questions, they are now more acute than ever and remain unsuitably answered. The disarray, which is especially—but not exclusively—affecting young people, is expressed in a number of symptoms of this *mal de vivre*.

"*Il est interdit d'interdire.*" (Forbidding is forbidden.)

One of the slogans of the student revolt in Paris, 1968

The signs of disarray have gradually appeared in the global society, producing fears and bringing young people together above differences of class, culture and country.

Rock music, gadgets and Coca-Cola have forged a new, parallel and temporary—as long as youth lasts—society and created what the African historian Joseph Ki-Zerbo calls "homo coca-colens." These new tribes constitute a global phenomenon. They are strongly attracted by the consumption society without, for the most part, having financial access to it.

Furthermore, their own perspective is an uncertain fight for survival in an unhospitable global society marked by gloomy perspectives such as brutal competition or the threat of unemployment.

As for their elders, many of them are inclined to return to traditional roots made of culture and religion, convinced, at least for the time being, that this will provide the only way out of a reality of misery and despair. In fact, another aspect of this great transition is the manifest need to come back to the spiritual principles such as those of Islam or Catholicism, or to find solace in cults and pseudoreligions. This is essentially the deep quest for the absolute, which is shared by so many human beings.

But in many cases, this need is perverted into fundamentalism and fanaticism, an expression of the immense disappointment vis-à-vis the Western model of modernization, consumption, economic growth and social progress which has never kept its promise in most developing countries, and has brought dehumanization in the industrialized regions.

Moreover, nationalism, which has always existed in various forms and degrees in all parts of the world, has now acquired a more vigorous dimension: in the Eastern European countries, for instance, the nationalist resurgence has been the driving force in the disintegration of Communist states, just as earlier, it was the most powerful lever in the anticolonial fights. But nationalism is double-edged: based on the old concept of the nation-state, it can all too easily become a source of intolerance, conflict and exaggerated racism.

The traditional concept of nation is partly disappearing in the wave of internationalization: dependence of some countries for raw materials and energy, dependence of others for food, investments, technology transfer and training are creating new solidarities that are not always yet accepted or understood.

The rebirth and reinforcement of xenophobia and racism can of course be explained by the millions of migrants in Asia, Africa, America and Europe who are felt to be a menace to the equilibrium of a country and a serious threat to its cultural identity just when this identity is being questioned by its own adepts. This phenomenon is all the more manifest in that it is induced by the vertigo of each individual facing the brutal emergence of the planeting dimension and the building of regional and interregional organisations such as the European Community, where people fear they will lose their soul.

These two opposing trends—the revival of specific cultural identities and the definition of vast, regional units—are in reality compatible. The apparent conflict arises from the difficulty of reconciling them within the existing political systems rigidly set within the model of the nation-state, which is unadapted to the present situation but also needs to be replaced by a solid cultural community. This is something very few are aware of.

Though this picture is rather grim, we can also point out that some positive signs are emerging. Young people are good at starting revolutions—no matter how soon they are co-opted—and it would be wrong to forget their role in the streets of Algeria, Africa, Chile, China, Rumania and the Soviet Union, just to mention a few.

The human malaise appears to be a normal stage of this great transition. Rebirth cannot take place immediately or without pain. It cannot disregard the diversity of societies and cultures, discount the burden of tradition or forget that words and concepts do not always have the same meaning in different languages. A quest such as this, for a new and more harmonious society, must not give in to the temptation of seeking unanimity by ignoring disagreements, or admit to defeat before the battle on seeing the perils of such an ambitious and difficult undertaking.

But the human malaise is also a reflection of the present dangerous march towards a schizophrenic world.

TOWARDS A SCHIZOPHRENIC WORLD

How can we speak of a global society when so many contradictory forces are exercising their power on societies and individuals, tossed about in a formidable hurricane?

We already have a foot in a two-world system which has replaced the three worlds we mentioned so facilely in our speeches, articles and reports. The three worlds—the industrialized one, the second one mainly constituted by the communist countries of Eastern Europe and the underdeveloped Third World—are no more.

The second world as such is disappearing. The Third World has exploded. Since Bandung and the movement of unaligned countries, is anything much left in common among the Asian Dragons and Bangladesh . . . and Haiti? Between Morocco and Burkina Faso? And in Brazil, between the wealthy industrialized region of Rio and Sao Paulo and the North East of the country suffering from starvation and malnutrition?

Diversities of interests are, of course, as obvious within countries and regions as on the international scene which concerns us here. Deep dichotomies existing in almost all countries, multiple standards of behaviour and hypocritical actions are much the same within as among nations, and reconciliation on the national scale would have to be sought as part of the global harmonization process.

In view of this we should note some of the unresolved areas of dichotomy and dispute most relevant to the world scene:

- the disparity between the rich and the poor with an increasing number of people living under the threshold of absolute poverty, less than U.S. $370 per year for 1 billion people in 1990;

- the growing disparity between those who have access to knowledge and information and those who do not;

- the discrimination against minorities, religious or ethnic, but also in so many countries against the old people;

- the absence of equal dispensation of social justice;

- lack of equivalence of rights and duties, of privilege and responsibility;

- the balance between discipline and licence;

- the ambiguity between economic growth and the quality of life;

- the caring community versus the impersonal welfare state;

- the lack of balance between material and spiritual needs.

Without trying to be exhaustive we should also mention a number of gaps that are contributing to the human malaise, for example the lack of understanding between the elites and the masses, the separation between science and culture or the conflict between rationality and intuition.

The areas of human difference are vast and have been hitherto regarded as irreconcilable. Differences of values and of ethical interpretation are present throughout the whole fabric of society and, once again, we have to reach the conclusion that only through the acceptance of an overriding common ethics of the survival of the race and the living planet can divergent interests be harmonized or, at least, mutual tolerance be achieved.

Most of the facets of this malaise are not new. But what makes them part of this first global revolution is the worldwide dimension that characterizes them, even if they exist to varying degrees, depending on the countries and the regions of the planet under consideration. There is no doubt but that the present trends and threats we are facing are induced by a state of mind inspired by both the globality of these situations, and the fears and aggressiveness of our contemporary fellow humans.

CONCLUSION:
THE CHALLENGE

NEVER IN THE COURSE OF HISTORY HAS HU-
mankind been faced with so many threats and dangers: catapulted unprepared into a world where time
and distance have been abolished, man is sucked into
a planetary cyclone swirling with seemingly unrelated factors, the causes and the consequences of
which form an inextricable maze. And yet we have,
in the preceding chapters, set out a number of facts,
the most important of which are: inequitable economic growth, governance and the capacity to govern, global food security and water availability,
environment and energy, population growth and migrations, the upheaval of world geostrategic facts.

All these factors are interdependent, interactive
and constitute what it has henceforth been agreed to
call the world problematique, according to the for-
mula launched by the Club of Rome.

Though public opinion has acquired a more or less
relative grasp of these facts, awareness of some of

them is all too often coupled with the ignorance of other no less important ones, as well as of the true breadth of each of them, and the interaction between them.

We must also note that the elements of the new problematique do not strike all people in the same way. Some, such as the dangers threatening environment, affect mankind as a whole. Others, such as the demographic explosion affecting the countries in the South, appear to be of more narrow concern but in reality have repercussions, to varying degrees of intensity, on every country in the world without exception.

Finally, at this coming turn of the century, mankind is overwhelmed by the scope of the phenomena coming at it from all sides, overwhelmed—and the word is not too strong—because the traditional structures, governments and institutions can no longer manage the problems in their present dimension. To make things worse, the archaic and unsuitable structures are set in a true moral crisis. The disappearance of value systems, the questioning of traditions, the collapse of ideologies, the absence of a global vision, the limits of the current practices of democracy confirm the void confronting societies. Individuals feel helpless, caught, as it were, between the rise of previously unknown perils on the one hand, and an incapacity to answer the complex problems in time and to attack the roots of evil, not just its consequences, on the other hand.

States with constitutional laws and rights violate international law anytime the matter is one of strict national interest. This is not really new but the magnitude of the consequences in an interdependent world is a totally new fact and globally totally visible. Religions often serve as an excuse for fratricidal strife: Christians massacre other Christians in Ireland or Lebanon without this having anything to do whatsoever with faith in the God of the Beatitudes. How can we not be concerned, along with many Arabs and Muslims, about the holy wars conducted in the name of Allah, which cast no more than a thin veil over the ambitions of war-chiefs who pay little heed to the teachings of the Koran? How can we not wonder, along with many Israelis, about the confusion of the religious mission of the People of Israel described in the Bible with the offensive annexation policy of governments shamelessly violating the United Nations laws to which they have subscribed, at least in writing?

The law of the jungle may be regressing, but the recent resurgence of its manifestations shows just how fragile world balance has remained. Such fragility lies also in the hearts and the minds of men, the oft impotent citizens of impotent nations. And we observe a general malaise with multifarious signs, striking men today with stupor, paralysis and unnamed fears.

Will we let ourselves be crushed by a problematique that seems superhuman, when we ourselves are at its root? Will we let ourselves be turned away from the real stakes and take refuge in a life on the margin of society, or in a quest for personal success and ignore our individual social responsibility?

Must we abandon ourselves to a sort of fatalism that would consider as inevitable or insurmountable the slow decline of humankind?

This is where the formidable challenge we are facing today lies. We shall now try to examine the possible responses to this challenge. A global challenge requires a global approach.

> "Time flies, our lives run out, and yet we are unable to overcome our insatiable urge for acquiring more and more worldly possessions."
>
> Sri Shankaracharya
> Eighth century
> Hindu philosopher, saint

II

THE
RESOLUTIQUE

INTRODUCTION

> "We must no longer wait for tomorrow; it has to be invented."
>
> Gaston Berger

WHAT IS OUR ABILITY TO TAKE EFFECTIVE ACTION?

Official vocabulary does not always suffice to define new situations and new technologies. We sometimes have no choice but to invent new words capable of expressing new concepts or new methodologies.

Such was the case for the "world problematique" launched by the Club of Rome when it was founded in 1968, and the force of facts has made it universal.

Since then, progressive awareness of a number of elements of the problematique has led to an unprecedented international phenomenon: increasing numbers of conferences, seminars and symposiums in the private as well as the public sector have been primarily devoted to the development of the poor countries.

The figures published by an official report of the Canton of Geneva read: "In 1977, 52,000 experts took part in 1,020 meetings on the Third World, representing 14,000 work sessions. The ad hoc meetings can be added to the regular day-to-day work of the 20,000 international civil servants of the 110 international organisations that have their headquarters in Geneva." We must also include the thousands of meetings held at the United Nations headquarters in New York, at the World Bank in Washington, at the European Community in Brussels, at the FAO[1] in Rome and in countless regional and subregional agencies in the developing countries. In thirteen years, there has been a runaway explosion of meetings of this sort and no one has ever totalled the budgets thus sunk into plane fares, luxury hotels and the publication and distribution of various and sundry reports and recommendations. Not only has little progress been observed on the field, but we must also acknowledge that poverty, famine and malnutrition have continued to increase in a great many of the countries in the South. An analogous phenomenon has been observed more recently where environmental problems are concerned, with a mind-boggling multiplication factor. It would not be correct, however, to judge that such meetings had no results and no beneficial effects.

Without being totally exempt from criticism in the matter, the Club of Rome became aware from one meeting to the next, with some meetings giving often

[1]United Nations Food and Agriculture Organisation.

debatable and sometimes even mediocre results, that it was no longer acceptable, at least as far as the Club was concerned, to speak of the problematique without worrying about actions that would tend to solve the problems set forth and analysed. The global approach to problems as expressed by the problematique implies a need for a corresponding global approach at every level of societies within a global perspective to interactive solutions destined to solve the problems. Therefore, a new methodology or better, a new enabling and purposeful analysis intended to be an answer to the world problematique is exactly what the Club of Rome means to adopt and call the world *resolutique.*

Bringing concrete solutions to the difficult problems of the great transition we are undergoing may very well be neither part of our capacities or our vocation, but it is our duty, at least unto ourselves, to search out ways to solutions and strategies for efficiency and equity. We must take initiatives intended to overcome situations that are blocked by international and national bureaucracies, by conventional and negative attitudes to change. Our task is also to encourage social and human innovation which, when compared to its cousin, technological innovation, is definitely a poor member of the family. We would like to emphasize once again that with the term *resolutique,* we are not suggesting a method to attack all the elements of the problematique in all its diversity and at the same time. This in any case would be impossible. Our proposal is rather a simultaneous attack on its main elements with, for each case, a careful consideration of reciprocal impacts from each of the others.

What are the values and goals on which action is based?

The world resolutique includes the need for adopting an ethical approach founded on the *collective values* that are sketchily emerging as a moral code for action and behaviour. Such codes and values have to constitute the source for international relations and the inspiration for decisions made by the main actors on this planet with due regard for cultural diversity and pluralism. But the resolutique also stresses the absolute necessity to seek concrete results in priority areas of the problematique, keeping in mind that the time factor is becoming essential. Any problem that remains unsolved produces in due time irreversible situations, some of which cannot even be solved in a global framework.

The Club of Rome and its individual members have always felt that beyond their research they had to take some operational-type initiatives or become associated with others. We can mention, for instance, the International Institute for Applied Systems Analysis (IIASA), the Foundation for International Training (FIT) or more recently, the International Partnership Initiative (IPI). We can also mention the Sahel Operation against desertification and in favour of development with the implication of the local populations, that was designed and launched on the request of a number of African leaders during the Club of Rome meeting at Yaoundé, Cameroon, in 1986.

The use of the resolutique applies to urgent action on priorities and immediacies. This does not exclude other types of action, which though not immediately necessary, can aim for much longer-term results. *In the shifting situations of the present, the need to develop methods of decision making in conditions of uncertainty is paramount.*

VII

THE THREE
IMMEDIACIES

THE MYRIAD STRANDS OF CHANGE WHICH together are constituting the world revolution have to be variously and severally understood, related, opposed, encouraged, diverted or assimilated. There can be no simple solution or packet of solutions to the tangle of inherent problems. Hence we introduce the concept of the resolutique, an approach which necessitates a simultaneous and comprehensive attack on all the problems *at every level,* coherent in that it attempts to look at the consequences of possible solutions to particular elements of difficulty, on all, or as many as possible, of the others. No comprehensive methodology exists for such an approach: it runs counter to traditional methods of planning, and existing institutional structures are singularly inappropriate for it. Yet there is no alternative. To tackle the global problematique problem by problem and on a country by country basis can only worsen the situation. The task that faces us, therefore, is to grasp a thousand nettles at the same time.

It is true that much thought has been given in recent years to the management of complexity, and some elements of approach have emerged. In particular, Jay Forrester's studies of large systems, described in his books, *Urban Dynamics*[1] and *Industrial Dynamics*,[2] which led to *The Limits to Growth*, have much to offer, as well as has *Les Systèmes du Destin*[3] by Jacques Lesourne.

> "In any complex system, attack—however apparently intelligent—on a single element or symptom, generally leads to a deterioration of the system as a whole."
>
> Forrester's First Law
> from an editorial in *The New York Times*

In introducing discussion of the elements that in differing patterns will constitute a possible resolutique, we start by considering three zones of the problematique which unquestionably demand immediate attack.

The first of these is the reconversion from a military to a civil economy. This assertion, which might have seemed perfectly realistic in the light of East–West detente and the substantial progress accomplished thanks to the negotiations conducted on disarmament by the Soviet Union and the United

[1]Forrester, 1969.
[2]Forrester, 1961.
[3]Lesourne, 1975.

States, seems to have been contradicted and made virtually absurd by the occurrence of the Gulf War. However, the Gulf War is precisely why the problems of disarmament and arms sales control are more than ever very much on the agenda. It is immediately pressing and seen as such by most governments and people. It is essentially a problem of transition.

The second theme is on global warming and the energy problems and is much more fundamental. As we have seen, delay in facing up to it could be tragic and catastrophic.

Third, there is the development issue. It raises all the problems of world poverty and disparities including failure to deal effectively with the external debt burden of the developing countries. It is urgent in the light of the relative failures of the past, the impasse, if not confrontation in the North–South dialogue and the need for new strategies and thinking if any sort of world harmony is to be achieved.

Guns and Butter; Swords and Ploughshares

The sudden ending of the cold war, the success already achieved towards disarmament and the prospects of still further reduction of both nuclear and conventional weapons has generated a degree of euphoria that the vast and wasteful global war machine can, to a large extent, be dismantled and resources redirected to constructive actions which the world so badly needs. While danger of world war has become less imminent but is not remote, local wars are raging in many places, so complete disarmament is unthinkable in our time. Indeed the Gulf war in the Middle East shows how easily the major powers can be dragged into a conflict, especially one which exposes their vulnerability to the withdrawal of the vital supplies which their hungry economies require. The prospect of a unified and strong Germany also raises historical doubts in both East and West.

Signs of the reality of the change are already visible: with agreement for the withdrawal of Soviet troops from Hungary and Czechoslovakia, for a halving of the British forces in Germany and the destruction in several countries of tanks and other military equipment, disarmament is on the march. The proposed Strategic Arms Reduction Talks (START) hope to reduce U.S. and U.S.S.R. strategic nuclear weapons by about one third and this is likely to be accompanied by big cuts in conventional forces in Europe, in terms of current proposals from 305,000 U.S. and 565,000 Soviet troops to 225,000 and 195,000, respectively.

These developments and the resource savings they bring are indeed welcome, but it has to be recognized that the huge military–industrial complex still exists with its vested interest in perpetuating military confrontation. National ministries and organisations of defence are inevitably disturbed at the prospect of the erosion of their high proportions of the national budget. This is largely concealed from public view by walls of secrecy. Military contractors, financed by the state and to a large extent protected from competition, are fearful of the future. In addition, the economies of a number of countries such as France and Czechoslovakia are heavily supported by arms exports. It has long been feared that if "peace breaks out" depression will follow. Global arms export is a significant element in international trade. In 1984 it reached a maximum of U.S. $57 billion, but then began to fall, owing to the economic difficulties in the developing countries to a mere (!) U.S. $47 billion in 1987. It should be noted that recently a few of the developing countries and in particular Brazil are themselves creating a capacity to manufacture and export arms. In a number of European countries such as Belgium and Austria, the prosperity of the arms industry depends essentially on export and is already suffering severe recession.

There is an understandable fear on the part of employees in the arms industries of the unemployment which would result from widespread disarmament. This could prove disastrous not only to individuals, but to company towns and whole regions in the main armament producing countries. This concern has been felt for many years in countries such as Great Britain where workers, groups and other activists, fearful of large-scale layoffs have advocated, so far with little success, policies of conversion to nonmilitary production. Certainly, even before a generalized disarmament could be anticipated, these fears were very real. First of all, there was a considerable over-capacity after the boom years of the mid-1980s. The second reason is that with greatly increased technical sophistication of the weaponry, it became more and more capital intensive and required fewer workers.

The partial liquidation of the arms industry thus brings many problems, and conversion of plants and of whole industries to production of consumer and other civilian goods has to be considered urgently. In the Soviet Union and China, large-scale demobilization and conversion efforts have been initiated as a matter of national policy and directed, as was to be expected, from the centre. In both these countries there is an enormous scarcity of consumer goods, agricultural machinery, medical equipment, machine tools and the like, so that conversion to the production of such goods was seen as highly desirable. Such endeavours have taken place in conditions of minimal public accountability and of economic chaos, giving little useful experience to countries operating the market economy. It is certain that the retraining of soldiers and armament workers to provide new skills and new attitudes is difficult and incomplete.

In contrast, in the Western market economy countries, only Sweden has as yet developed an active policy of conversion; most of the others have adopted a wait-and-see attitude. Nevertheless, the conversion issue is being discussed actively in most European countries except for France, despite the fact that much of its weapons manufacturing capacity, mostly state owned, is already idle.

Conversion of arms plants to civil construction is thus the currently accepted remedy, but this, in the industrialized countries, presents many difficulties. Existing laissez-faire attitudes assume that the market forces will take care of the transition. This may be so, but the consequences are likely to be the waste of abandoned and unwanted plants and extensive unemployment. State manufacturing facilities and contractors that have served the needs of the military for long are often incapable of operating new manufactures in a market environment. Grass-roots action on the part of employees, trade unions, local communities, etc., holds out some hope in some countries, but is unlikely to secure sufficient institutional backing in the absence of clear governmental policies. Directly interventionalist action is unlikely and would, in any case, be inappropriate as a consequence of bureaucratic rigidity. Yet an active role is called for in view of the serious nature of the priority changes involved. The success of any comprehensive conversion scheme will depend heavily on the availability of extensive retraining facilities which only governments can provide. It may well be that governments will be forced to action by the pressure of public opinion and grass-roots agitation. This is another example of the need for people's power.

The question must now be raised as to what the products of the converted industries should be. Unlike the Eastern European countries and China, which have great shortages of consumer and civilian goods, the Western countries have a manufacturing overcapacity and market saturation, so that indiscriminate conversion would merely deepen existing economic problems and structural unemployment. The overriding need, therefore, is to be clear about the objectives of the new economy, taking account of the possibilities of industrial renewal which the advanced technologies can provide, the environmental constraints, increasing social demands for better housing and medical care and the need to create employment. Conversion policies can only succeed if viewed comprehensively. A simplicist approach which would convert warplane manufacture to that of commercial aircraft, tank factories to automobile plants and warship and submarine yards to the construction of unwanted merchant shops and tankers would be economically catastrophic and contribute both to earth-warming and the human malaise. Wise statesmanship is needed here to view the situation in its totality. Conversion is simply not enough; it is but one element in the reconstruction of industry to meet the needs of humanity.

In brief, disarmament entails fairly high immediate and near-term costs, as it becomes increasingly evident that industrial capacity set up for defence purposes cannot easily be adjusted to supplying long-delayed ordinary civilian consumption needs.

We have as yet said little here about how the savings of money and resources which are expected to flow from disarmament should be used. The claims are innumerable and obvious—the satisfaction of national needs for social improvement, protection of the environment, elimination of poverty, aid to development. These are just a few of the candidates. It is probable, however, that much of the financial gain will go rather to tax reduction and the liquidation of national debt. Public expectations for a "disarmament dividend" are unlikely to be fully met.

A few words must be said about a special case, namely the reconversion or retention of power and influence of the many scientists and research engineers who formed the hidden core of armaments research and development. At the height of the armaments race it was estimated that almost half of the world's research physicists and engineers were engaged in military activities. These were the key people whose work created ever-more sophisticated weapons. Although locked in intellectual rivalry, the scientists of the two sides in the cold war formed a sort of unholy alliance in thinking up new methods of destruction and ever-increasingly accurate delivery mechanisms. The military strategists and the armies had to follow their lead into a bewildering technological nightmare, impenetrable even by the decision-making politicians. These scientists were isolated behind walls of secrecy. They lived and worked outside the international scientific community. Although they must include many of the best brains of science, their names are largely unknown. Unlike other scientists, rewards and prestige did not come from sense of achievement and respect of their peers in the international scientific community but from competitive success within their restricted circle.

What then is to happen to these people in a situation of disarmament? Will they be converted and join the ranks of academic and industrial scientists, or will they remain at their work, devising still more deadly weapons, hopefully never to be used. It is too early to say, but to date the latter seems to be the most likely option, probably with decreasing employment and resources. The 1990 yearbook of SIPRI (the authoritative Stockholm International Peace Research Institute) asserts that there is no evidence that there will be a slower pace of technological change in the military area. This key element of the armament system is largely outside public scrutiny and concern. Because it withdraws so many of the best scientific and engineering brains from fully creative activity, it is important that it be discussed and the situation rendered visible.

In conclusion on this theme, we summarize some suggestions for action.

Fear of nuclear war between the superpowers has

receded, but limited use of chemical, biological and nuclear weapons in local wars remains an alarming possibility. It is widely believed that several countries already possess a hidden nuclear capacity. We call therefore for a new appeal *for adherence to the non-proliferation treaty*, its signature and willingness on the part of the signatories to accept international inspection. We also plead for a speeding up of negotiations aimed at burning research and the use of chemical and biological weapons.

In view of recent agreements on disarmament and the prospect of further progress we appeal to all governments with sizeable but declining arms industries to institute *active policies for reconversion* of these. Can we hope that this reconversion will be to the manufacture of products that will contribute to the health and welfare of their people? Such policies should be evolved and implemented with the advice of bodies which include progressive industrialists (and not only those from armament manufacture) together with workers' representatives and government officials. The conversion policies should be shaped in full recognition of the changing nature of industry and with due regard to the constraints imposed by earth-warming and other environmental hazards. In all such schemes an essential element should be the setting up of retraining schemes to fit workers with the necessary new skills.

In considering the *redeployment* of financial and other resources set free by diminished military expenditure, governments should give priority to the improvement of the social structure. In particular great efforts are required to improve the quality of education to provide their citizens with the knowledge and skills necessary to allow fulfillment in work, leisure in the new world which is emerging. In the striving for world harmony, part of the resources should be used to augment existing assistance to development and the alleviation of world poverty.

The present, historical situation of detente should be used to make visible and *curtail the evils of the arms trade.* In 1986, the President of the Club of Rome on the basis of a memorandum by Eduard Pestel sent to President Reagan and General Secretary Gorbachev a proposal for joint action of the two superpowers to limit the sale of arms to the poorer countries. While there was only a formal acknowledgment from the White House, a personal and constructive reply was sent by Mr. Gorbachev, followed by a memorandum of further reflection. The correspondence was given full coverage by the press and TV in the Soviet Union and Eastern Europe but was hardly noticed by the press in the West. It seems to us that the time is ripe to revive this proposal, not only with the United States and the Soviet Union, but with other major arms exporting countries. Recent events demonstrate the futility of the "evil trade" and how it can have a lethal backlash when the turn of events gives rise to unforeseen conflicts. One has only to cite the success of the French-manufactured Exocet missiles in sinking British battleships during the Falklands War, or the situation with the troops of Western and Arab countries in Saudi Arabia, facing sophisticated Iraqi weapons sold to them by the Russians, the French and the British among others. To sell guns for immediate monetary gain to buyers who may intend to kill the seller seems to be an ultimate insanity.

Special attention and visibility should be given to the situation of *military research and development* as described above.

In the long run, if the security of the planet is to be assured, the manufacture of arms for the economic gain of individuals or countries will have to be controlled. Residual needs for world policing will have to be provided under the authority of the United Nations. This may not be for tomorrow; nevertheless, there is a need for an early review of the whole problem, all the more so that the confrontations in the Persian Gulf will have long-term consequences.

Towards an Environment for Survival

Most of the successful activity of recent years for the protection of the environment has been in reducing or eliminating pollution and other forms of deterioration; it has been curative rather than preventive. While this must continue, the main emphasis in the future must be in preventing the development of the macropollutions which we have described earlier to the level at which their effects are irreversible. By far the most urgent of these is Earth-Warming which threatens the global economic and social system.

Prevention of this represents one of the greatest challenges which humanity has faced, and demands a total and international effort. Four paths of attack are required:

- Reduction of the global emission of carbon dioxide which will necessitate less use of fossils fuels;

- Reforestation, especially in the tropics;

- Development of alternative forms of energy;

- Conservation of energy and development of greater efficiency in its use.

We shall base our discussion of the carbon dioxide situation on the Toronto "changing atmosphere" target of the need to reduce emission of this gas by 20% by the year 2005. However, in accepting the urgent need of the developing countries to provide energy for their citizens, their agriculture and their industries, the industrialized countries will have to make even larger percentage reductions in their use of fossil fuels—let us say 30%. Moreover, recent estimates indicate that this is a very conservative figure.

Initially, the highest priority must be given to energy conservation and efficiency in the transmission and use of energy in every sector of the economy. There are very large potential savings to be made which would in any case be economically useful and strategically necessary in view of the vulnerability of the industrial countries to the cutting off of oil supplies. In general, the market forces should be helpful here, but at present incentives are insufficient and will have to be increased. There are also many nonmarket barriers to energy conservation. In the domestic sector, for example, it is noticeable that per capita consumption of energy in the United States and Canada is about double that of the Western European countries with an approximately equivalent standard of living. To achieve the necessary savings here will require fundamental changes in the habits of millions of individuals, a question to which we shall return later.

The immediate need, therefore, is for the launching of a massive and worldwide campaign to promote energy conservation and efficiency of use. This alone can give us some breathing space in order to face up to the more intractable problems of industrial adjustment. To be successful it will need a clearly expressed political will on the part of governments and strong public support.

Switching from oil and coal to other energies is also suggested, but there are few alternatives which could be brought into use quickly, apart from natural gas. This has the advantage that the methane molecule in combustion produces less CO_2 per unit of energy generated as compared with the longer chain hydrocarbons of oil and coal. Conversion to natural gas is relatively simple, so this may be a useful measure, although great care would have to be taken to prevent leakage, since methane is itself a greenhouse gas, molecule by molecule, much more active than carbon dioxide.

These are, however, only palliatives or delaying *measures*. The fundamental issue is how to secure a massive reduction of fossil fuel combustion in industry. It is frequently stated that transition to the post-industrial society will lead to considerable energy saving. It is true that the microelectronic technologies are not energy-intensive, but their main applications are in the growing important information sector, rather than in heavy industry, where, through control techniques, they can contribute greatly to energy efficiency. We have to remember that in an information-dominated society we shall still need heavy goods, chemicals and other traditional manufactures, just as agricultural demand was still needed after the Industrial Revolution had taken over.

Reduction of fossil fuel use by industry, at least in the short and medium terms, requires either considerable technological innovation both in manufacturing methods and in the energy efficiency of those in present use, or else a drastic reduction of industrial activity. This would necessitate a radical reorientation of the economy taking into account the intricate relationships of economic activity, ecology and technology. This is not a task which governments can be expected to do effectively: it calls for new forms of government–industry co-operation. Here the Japanese model may have something to contribute to the West.

A number of European countries, notably Norway, Sweden and the Netherlands, are already discussing these problems seriously and determining targets for their national contributions towards reduction of the global CO_2. Sweden, for example, has a requirement to maintain CO_2 emissions at the 1988 level, while retaining its policy of phasing out nuclear power. How these targets can be achieved is another matter. These initiatives are indeed a useful start and similar exercises are needed in other countries. Co-ordinated effort also exists at the international level and is already under study in the EEC. The social as well as the economic consequences of a drastic cutting back of industrial activity are mind-boggling and will be taken up later.

In their own interest, the developing countries will have to share the burden of stabilizing the global climate, and their influence in this will increase rapidly with demographic and industrial growth. Development in these countries will inevitably increase energy demand, and much of this can only be in the form of fossil fuels. Increased use of biomass through new biotechnologies is to be hoped for. But we must remember that this too generates carbon dioxide. Again increased numbers will mean greater use of fuelwood for domestic purposes, and the burning of wood has a greater greenhouse effect than that of coal. Energy efficiency is thus also of primary importance to the developing countries. So far, industrialization in these countries has been set by the path of the industrialized countries of the North. If things continue in this direction, the results will be disastrous for the countries in question and for the world as a whole. It is therefore important that the improved cleaner technologies that the industrialized countries are striving for are made freely accessible to the developing world and incentives given for their adoption as well as aid in their implementation.

So far we have concentrated on carbon dioxide, the classic greenhouse gas, but we have to remember that a whole range of other minor components of the atmosphere contribute to about an equal extent in the effect. Methane is one of the most important, and its origin in the air requires much more knowledge from research. Oxides of nitrogen are also critical. Their main source is from agriculture and especially from the present excessive use of fertilizers. This also raises the question of energy use in agriculture, which has increased greatly in recent decades. There is a pressing need for the agricultural authorities to take up the question of making their industry much less energy-intensive and of reverting to more organic systems. This is desirable also in the expectation that oil prices and hence nitrogenous fertilizers will be much more costly in the future.

> "Whatever I dig from thee, Earth, may that have quick growth again. O purifier, may we not injure thy vitals or thy heart."
>
> Hymn to the Earth
> Atharva Veda (3000 B.C.)

We have already stressed the need to bring a halt to the elimination of the forests as the second path to CO_2 reduction. It is estimated that, for the world as a whole, a quarter of the carbon dioxide emissions originate from deforestation; within the developing countries taken as a whole, it is one half; in Latin America and some parts of South East Asia it is as great as three quarters. While responsibility is essentially that of the countries where the vanishing forests exist, most of the demand comes from the rich countries, so a solution has to be sought in co-operative approaches, supported by international funds.

It is important that flagrant cases of destructive resource policies should be subjected to international discipline. This applies, for example to Japanese activities of deforestation and whaling. Recently, Columbia has put forward an imaginative proposal for the stabilization of the ecological condition of the Amazonian basin, by joint action of the countries of the region—Brazil, Columbia, Peru and Venezuela. Such a scheme would involve international financing and deserves urgent consideration.

We return briefly to the general question of the availability of alternative sources of energy. Our conviction is that unless sufficient clean energy can be developed during the next few decades, it will be difficult, if not impossible to sustain societies at the levels now enjoyed by the present industrialized countries and at the same time make possible an acceptable standard of living in the developing world. As already stated, prospects are not bright, but undoubtedly new possibilities would arise if concerted world efforts are made through research and development on the scale of the effort to put a man on the moon, or the Manhattan Project during the Second World War. Motivation for doing so should be very much greater than for these two projects and should attract universal support. This would include efforts to provide soft energies such as solar economically and in quantity, and here the developing countries, largely bountifully endowed with sunlight, could play a big part. We suggest, with the greatest reluctance, that the nuclear fission option should be kept open as being probably less dangerous than the combustion of oil or coal. In a situation of ecological crisis, with the need for drastic reduction of carbon dioxide emission and with quite insufficient clean fuel availability, nuclear power could help to close the energy gap. However, even if accepted, the time required to put new nuclear power stations into commission would limit the nuclear component to a relatively small, even if critically important proportion of the necessary fossil-fuel replacement.

A few words should be added here on the undervalued significance of energy in human transactions. Energy is, after all, the only absolute. Through the

Einstein equation, matter and energy are equivalent. Energy assessment we now see as an essential tool in evaluating new technologies and hence the nature of societies. Energy accounting is becoming increasingly necessary in measuring, for example, the carrying capacity of countries for human and animal populations, or the viability of human and other systems. The belief that monetary management or even manipulation can lead to a proper accounting and evaluation of growth and development needs to be eradicated. Energy, on the other hand is the driving force in the economy; money is simply its surrogate. There is surely a strong argument at this stage of human development to devise a new economics based on the flow of energy. We hear many proposals for energy taxation suggested by present difficulties. These demand consideration. Also interesting proposals have been made for energy to be used as the basis for general taxation, both national and local. Many possibilities are opening up in this new field, and the Club of Rome has proposed study on the various suggestions for energy taxation for the purpose of controlling the energy in the North and of insuring that in the South development should be on the basis of clean energy.

In conclusion on this theme, we summarize some suggestions for action.

It is urgent that a *Worldwide Campaign of Energy Conservation and Efficiency* be launched. To be successful, this will require that world leaders express strongly their conviction that it is necessary and show the political will to implement it. It would be appropriate that the scheme be launched by the United Nations in association with the United Nations Environment Programme, the World Meteorological Organisation and UNESCO. A corollary would be the setting up in each country of an *Energy Efficiency Council* to supervise the operation on the national scale.

The global nature as well as the seriousness of the environmental threats and especially that of earth-warming indicates the need for a coherent and comprehensive attack at the international and presumably United Nations level. We require much more knowledge of the complexities of the natural system and specifically of the detailed mechanism of the greenhouse and ozone depletion effects. Equally, indications of the probable impact of these and other phenomena on the future climate of particular regions are urgently necessary. We are not convinced, however, that these research, development and monitoring requirements argue for the creation of yet another UN agency. The need could be met by strengthening the existing agencies, especially those mentioned above, and giving them a mandate to cooperate together in a jointly planned, comprehensive programme of research.

Even more urgent is the need to create a competent high-level body to consider in depth and over a long time frame the implications of the macropollution phenomena on economy, society and the individual. In view of the multidisciplinary nature of the many facets of this problem and the complexity of the interactions between them, it is hard to see how this could be accomplished effectively in the conventional manner, by a group of political personalities sitting in New York. We suggest, therefore, that the opportunity be taken to break with institutional tradition in creating a group of outstanding political figures yes, but reinforced by individuals from industry, economy and science. It is not sufficient that a group consisting exclusively of politicians should be charged with this task, so vital for the future of humanity, no matter how well briefed they might be by scientists and others in their various countries. It is necessary for independent experts to sit with them around the table. Churchill did not get it quite right when he said that "scientists should be on tap but not on top."

Security is no longer exclusively a matter of the prevention of war. Irreversible environmental destruction is becoming a threat to World Security of the same order of magnitude. To meet the needs expressed above, we therefore reiterate the recommendation of the Club of Rome declaration of 1989 that a world conference on the common environmental imperatives be called, aimed at the creation of a *UN Environmental* Security Council parallel to the existing Security Council on military matters. This body would not be restricted to the members of the existing Security Council, but would have strong representation of the developing countries as well as the nonpolitical members suggested above, who would take an active part in the discussions, but would not, however, be voting members. If not constituted earlier, this could be a major outcome of the United Nations Conference on Environment and Development to be held in Brazil in 1992.

In addition, we propose the organisation, possibly under the auspices of the Environmental Security

Council, of regular meetings of industrial leaders, bankers and governments of the five continents. These *Global Development Rounds,* envisaged as somewhat similar to the Tariff Rounds of GATT, would consider the need to harmonize competition and cooperation in the light of environmental constraints.

The problems of industrial adjustment to the lessened use of fossil fuels necessitates the drawing up of national strategies to respect the quota contribution of each country to global CO_2. This will involve also consideration of how to design modified process and equipment, and the stimulation of research and development programmes for clean energy systems. We propose, therefore, the creation, particularly in the highly industrialized countries, of *National Centres for Clean Technology.* These might well be organised in association with the national energy efficiency councils proposed above.

The urgent need for an intensive effort to develop alternative energy sources to replace partially the use of the fossil fuels demands an immediate and massive world effort of an equal magnitude to the American grand scheme for placing a man on the moon. We recommend, therefore, that the United Nations, either directly or through a group of its agencies and programmes, should convene an intergovernmental scientific meeting to plan a comprehensive *World Alternative Energy Project.* This would entail considerable financial resources, with the various elements of an internationally agreed programme carried out by the most appropriate "centres of excellence" in the world, irrespective of the country in which they are situated. The matter is so important to the world, and the need to employ the best brains and equipment so essential, that all principles of a national quid pro quo between contributions and benefits would have to be excluded. A network building on the existing centres of excellence is much to be recommended in contrast to the construction of a simple international centre with the inevitable rigidities and bureaucracies. The nuclear fission option should be kept open as an emergency measure to meet energy requirements during the transition.

The Food and Agriculture Organisation, FAO, should be invited in association with the Consultative Group of Institutes of Agricultural Research (CGIAR) to undertake a study on *Energy in Agriculture* with a view to recommending means of reducing energy inputs in agriculture and, at the same time, of lessening agriculture's emission of greenhouse gases.

All these measures or the equivalent cannot be implemented unless the public is well informed and understands the consequences of inaction. It is necessary, therefore, that concepts of global development including the issues of industrialization be integrated into *educational programmes*, to include instruction on environmental protection, energy and resource saving, the preservation of cultural values and many other aspects. We therefore call on UNESCO, Ministers of Education, parents associations, television authorities and others to undertake this essential task.

Development Versus Underdevelopment

The third immediacy is a crucial element in the first global revolution. The present situation of a number of countries of the Southern hemisphere is in a state of constant deterioration for a number of causes we will analyze further on.

According to World Bank estimates (1990), 1 billion human beings in those countries are presently living under the threshold of absolute poverty—with an income of less than U.S. $370/year—as opposed to 500 million in the early 1980s. There is reason to believe that the aggravation of underdevelopment, poverty, famine and malnutrition will continue throughout the coming years despite the constitution of exceptional zones of development.

Here it is important to keep in mind the different economic levels from which countries started out since, as has been stressed in this book, it is no longer correct to treat the so-called Third World as homogeneous.

In particular, our concern is with the least-developed nations, most of which are in Africa, and many of which gained their independence from the colonial powers only in the post–World War II period; thus, they had either to start from scratch or to attempt to convert a highly dependent colonial economic structure into one which had to be oriented more clearly to domestic needs and national interests. This entailed diversifying both exports and sources of financial support.

The NICs (New Industrialized Countries) of Asia have had a different experience, based on a separate strategy, and have been remarkably successful in adapting to the world economy and in raising their own living standards. Other countries, particularly India and China, have quite different characteristics from the least developed countries and those of the Pacific Rim dynamic market economies. The Latin

American countries with a long history of independence are nevertheless highly dependent on trade in
basic commodities. At the same time, in several major
cases, they are undergoing rapid industrialization.
Among the Latin American countries, a few notably
weak economies are close to the least developed. This
is also true in the small island states of the Carribean.

**Inadequacies of Development Policies in the Past Twenty
Years** A large number of the least developed economies was encouraged to start out by adopting huge
industrial and infrastructural projects involving high
construction costs on the capital-intensive Western
model. They seriously neglected basic rural and small
industrial development that could have brought immediate benefit to large sectors of the population, instead of to small minorities. Many of those large
investments have failed in their objectives. Policies
adopted from the Western industrial countries have
often clashed with local customs and structures and
induced rejection by the very people they were supposed to benefit. People-oriented development was
traditionally set aside, in favour of projects that only
rich countries could afford. Not only was it the result
of the desire of leaders to achieve extremely rapid
transformation of their economies and societies, but
it was aided, abetted and often proposed by international agencies and bilateral North–South programmes.

Such policies have resulted in a long series of projects which, among other things, have plunged many
countries into debt and financial disorder, with little
solid benefit. Outstanding have been the large dams,
of which Aswan in Egypt is a leading example, al-

though many more could be mentioned in Africa, Asia and Latin America. There has been a catalogue of disasters, with past lessons being neither learned nor understood: hundreds of thousands of people have been displaced without any previously prepared settlements to receive them; waterborne epidemic diseases have been disseminated; local environment has been disrupted. The frequent ecological and human disasters subsequent to these large projects have often caused unprecedented financial waste. Macroprojects such as Itaipu in Brazil and the Narmada project in India are also telling examples. Iron and Steel, petrochemical and shipbuilding installations, have mainly proved uneconomic and have come under much criticism. Most of these projects have also given too little consideration to environmental implications, to the effect upon displacement, manpower needs, maintenance and so on.

In many cases, even in the semi-industrialized countries, industrial development based on import-substitution policies requiring extremely high tariff and nontariff protection has produced heavy disparities between the modern sectors and the traditionally poor rural sectors, from which populations have drifted to the big cities as cheap labor. Often they have merely joined the already vast number of urban "marginal" settlers living in subhuman conditions.

"Hunger is ashamed of no one and does not fear God. Only organised and conscious work can make it retreat."

A Farmer in Burkina Faso

The People of the Slums, the Favellas and the Bidonvilles
The urban population of developing countries went from 90 million in 1900 to nearly 1 billion in 1985 and has been rising at a rate of over 40 million per year.

Two-thirds of the population of Latin America is urbanized while urbanization in Africa increased from a ratio of 5% in 1900 to 25% in 1985. Sixty-one percent of the world's city population live in Asia, where the evolution of the rate of urbanization is comparable to that of developed countries. According to the latest United Nations estimates, the number of city-dwellers will have reached about 2 billion by the year 2000, with a 109% increase in Africa, 50% in Latin America and 65% in Asia. There are a number of reasons for this.

Rural depopulation is constantly bringing into the outskirts of the large cities streams of people driven from their land by poverty and the impossibility of survival, but also as a result of local wars (some twenty in Africa alone), large infrastructural projects requiring the displacement of the population, etc.

It is important to accept, however, that although rural depopulation in favour of big cities can be slowed down, it can certainly not be stopped. A first reason is that cities exercise a powerful attraction on the younger rural population wishing to flee an unbearable poverty; for these youngsters cities with their relative modernity represent hope. Another reason is that any progress in the area of agricultural production deprives a growing percentage of young people of their work. As it happened in Western countries, they go to the cities, in the hope of finding a new kind of work, even if it is only small trades.

The true fascination exercised by the big cities on people, young and not-so-young, is based on a set of rational and irrational motivations.

As Mattei Dogan and John D. Kasarda wrote in *A World of Giant Cities:*[4]

> The cities act like a gigantic Las Vegas in the sense that the bulk of their populations are gamblers, though the games are different. Instead of roulette or black-jack, their names are job security, individual social mobility, better access to education for the children and hospitals for the sick. Wonderful stories circulate about the happy few who made it in a big way.

However, confrontation, whether softly expressed or violent, is growing between the poor and the rich in developing countries. The Western model is denounced, yet at the same time envied and hated because of the impossibility of attaining it. The hatred of the poor for the rich is aimed mainly at the West and especially at its most blatant form in the image of the wealth and waste of American society as viewed on television. But it is also focused on the ostentation, arrogance and life-styles of local elites.

City governments have so far been unable to con-

[4]Dogan and Kasarda, 1988.

trol the flow and to provide adequate integration structures, health and education services, for a new underclass that is vulnerable to all kinds of diseases and can sink into all sorts of marginal behaviour such as prostitution and drug-dealing.

The Need for Population Policies   We turn again to the central issue of the population explosion which must have its place in the resolutique. As already stated, in many countries there is a grim race between population growth and development. So much economic improvement, achieved at the expense of so much human effort, is consumed by increasing numbers. In hindsight, one can only muse about how prosperous countries such as India, so well endowed by nature, would be today had they been able to maintain their early twentieth-century populations.

There is undoubtedly an urgent need for these countries to adopt sensible and human policies of population regulation, encouraging family-planning measures to complement the death-control achievements ushered in by improved medicine and hygiene. One of the surest means of attaining lower fertility rates is through the spontaneous processes that follow economic improvement, but in many places this is a far-off hope, made even more distant by the high rate of population growth, thus casting the whole issue into a vicious circle.

A scientific breakthrough in contraceptive technology is also long overdue, especially cheap and widely available oral or other contraceptives which would greatly facilitate population control. Also the direct correlation between fertility and female illiteracy needs urgent attention.

Population control, necessary as it is, must be planned in terms of human well-being. It is of paramount importance that all countries striving for development should design their population policies. These policies have to be based on detailed exploration of the demographic growth prospects in relation to resource availability and development aims, including the standard of living which each country hopes to achieve. Only through informed assessment of such prospects can development planning be realistic. If the public is to respond to population control needs, it must be given sufficient information to understand the dangers of overpopulation for the individual and the benefits that would flow from population growth restraint. Such conditions are necessary if population planning is to be implemented with humanity.

The Need for New Strategies of Development It is clearly necessary to rethink development policies and practices. Much greater priority has to be given to the needs of the marginalized and forgotten millions of the rural poor in all parts of the underdeveloped world. It is necessary also to go back to first base and question the underlying assumption of most development policies, namely that the economic success of the presently industrialized countries, achieved through the systematic pursuit of a technology-based economic growth, is the inevitable path to be followed by all countries and all cultures. The newer generations in many countries, while by no means rejecting the need for modernization and material improvement, insist on the need to draw on their own traditions and skills in creating their own patterns of development.

Imitation is not enough. It is more important for such countries to construct their own capacities for scientific research and technological transfer. In a period of rapid scientific and technological change in the industrialized countries, the importation of traditional methods of manufacture can lead industrialization to obsolescence. It is remarkable that in many countries that boast of modern industry and services, malnutrition and illiteracy are widely prevalent, with a large percentage of the population in a condition of extreme poverty.

Some of these cases have been near-catastrophic with inequality and poverty actually worsened. It is clear that global development cannot continue along these lines, and that a serious reconsideration of development strategies is absolutely necessary. A reversal of these trends also implies radical change in the political systems, stability, elimination of corruption, a setting of priorities based on the needs of future generations, and strong limitations to the abusive spread of bureaucracies.

In the semi-industrialized countries, especially in those that became heavily indebted during the 1970s and 1980s, the adjustments they have had to make to maintain service of their external debt and to reduce inflation and waste have forced them to cancel large projects, to redesign their strategies, and, particularly, to reduce the scope of the public sector and provide strong incentives instead to domestic private entrepreneurs. An important role can be played by direct foreign investment in this process. Many of these countries have had no alternative but to create conditions under which their industries must become internationally competitive, following to some extent the experience of the Pacific Rim countries. This process has gone on sometimes at the expense of the domestic market and with great sacrifice in terms of employment and regular salaried incomes.

We cannot ignore that in many countries, especially in Africa south of the Sahara, too low a priority has been given to agricultural improvement. This is due partly to inflated hopes of what might be expected from industrialization and partly due to the fact that industries arise mainly in or near cities. In unstable political situations, danger to the authorities is generated mainly in the urban environment. Disturbance and insurrection can easily be incited among the masses of the insufficiently employed poor. Rural opposition on the other hand is widely dispersed over the countryside and thus difficult to organise. The temptation, therefore, is to invest in development projects that promise employment and stability in the urban areas. The consequence of insufficient agricultural investment has been a main obstacle in the race between food production and population growth.

Rural development remains an unquestionable priority because the whole population, rural and urban, has to be fed and countries aim to become food self-sufficient.

It must be strongly emphasized that the problem of the organisation of the international market of raw materials has yet to be solved. It is of prime importance to find a way to ensure that the price of raw materials not be fixed by international markets to the benefit of industrialized countries and to the detriment of developing ones.

Local Initiatives   Both in the North and in the South, in spite of heavy handicaps of many sorts, it is remarkable that the willpower of small groups of men and women has managed to start moving towards the achievement of improvements for the lower income strata based on their own efforts, with appropriate assistance from central and local governments, international agencies, domestic and foreign nongovernmental organisations, and new bilateral programmes.

The Club of Rome undertook a large survey on the role of local initiatives in the rural areas.[5] We focus on this field knowing that parallel initiatives in handicrafts and small manufactures and in the urban outskirts are also very effective and shall be encouraged. Large numbers of small development projects in agriculture, health and education have sprung up in the poorest parts of Latin America, Africa and Asia, initiated by NGOs, independent organisations, farmers groups, village communities. According to estimates made in 1985, over 100 million farmers were involved in development projects headed by one or several NGOs. The movement is growing rapidly.

Today, NGOs in the South exist by the thousands in India, the Philippines and South America and by the hundreds in Africa, Indonesia and Thailand. And although their histories are different, they are joined in a common effort, with few resources and some

[5]Schneider, 1988.

backing from NGOs in the North, to meet needs that are the same everywhere, and above all the basic needs of food, clean water and hygiene. They are also enabling village dwellers to realize what their problems are and engage in a situation where they can take responsibility for their own development. This means getting organised and trained, and getting everyone involved including women, outcasts and the disabled. It means making progress by digging wells or building tanks to collect rainwater for irrigation, improving the quality of seed and livestock, planting trees, building latrines, educating children and saving. Local savings, mostly due to women, are a fundamental investment for the future that should be particularly developed. Throughout all of this, in fact, we can never overestimate the essential, irreplaceable part women are playing in development all over the world.

NGO and volunteer agency actions have made a decisive and vital contribution, especially in the poorer regions of the world. There is no doubt that these actions will spread, for word about the villages that have come back to life gets around very quickly, reaching even the most distant villages in the desert, jungle or mountain. And villagers who were thought to be inert, fatalistic and resigned—when in fact they usually had no hope and were too hungry to act—are beginning to believe that it can work for them too and are finding the will to improve their own lot and build a better future for their children.

Priority must therefore be given in many places to small-scale projects, properly integrated into a global strategy.

To avoid the financial waste and unwanted consequences of the large-scale projects we previously mentioned, to make the best of the lessons derived from their experience, it seems necessary to reverse the process that has been engaged in so far and start out by favouring small-scale projects needing far lesser investments and resulting in progress that is beneficial to the majority of people.

At a time when financial resources are becoming even scarcer, the current situation demands that NGOs in the North, and even more so the international agencies and financial institutions, review the policies they have applied so far. Concretely, part of the investments planned for large-scale projects should be transferred to finance small-scale projects. The advantage of the latter is that they train the local men and women and set up the structures—village communities, farmers' associations—to launch a development based on the people's own needs and options, implemented with their active involvement and under their responsibility. The replicability of the projects from village to village is starting to have a multiplying effect on the progress of development of groups of villages, then of regions.

Beyond a certain stage of this kind of development, medium-scale works like roads, markets, small hospitals, schools become indispensable. Thus villages and NGOs have no choice—even though it may seem difficult—but to pursue their action in a concerted movement with government policies. In the same way, creation of home industries, small business firms or handicraft enterprises are set up and give access to new productions and therefore new modest incomes.

The Role of Governments This global vision of rural development based on new perspectives and priorities requires full recognition of the role of local initiatives and the so-called NGOs by governments. In fact, if a government decides to implement a rural development policy, this assumes that it has made essential political choices that must in many instances include land-reform, population policy and development of small-scale health facilities. However, recognition of the effectiveness of NGOs by governments remains often rather theoretical.

Again and again it has been observed how the results of small-scale projects can be compromised by the application of practices and even policies that are in contradiction to the type of development they stood for. Purchase prices for farm products do not sufficiently remunerate farmers' work and discourage instead of encouraging them. Similarly, direct and indirect taxes on the national level are bitterly felt in rural areas, where income is generally very low. Government taxation with its resulting financial strangulation could well slow down or put a stop to all small-scale project efforts, whatever outside financial aid there is.

When governments have decided to support this approach to rural development, they must then modify their political and financial options and adopt a policy of higher buying prices for villagers, as well as relieving some of the tax pressure.

Rural development based on small-scale projects also demands that governments implement national planning policies favouring road-construction and the development of intermediate settlements between villages and big towns.

The absence of roads excludes a large number of village communities from normal trading and makes them live in a "closed circuit." Some of them have built roads or bridges themselves, but they are not equipped for such tasks, which should be planned on a national level and carried out on the basis of a systematic policy. Similar problems arise in the area of primary and secondary school education, hospitals, some higher-level training and leisure activities for the young. As we just pointed out, there is no intermediate level between the village and the big towns.

Moreover, corruption must be fought at every level of the state, and this implies among other measures the training of lower-level civil servants to motivate and involve them in a development policy well understood as a national priority.

We shall argue later that a major need in the development of the South is the creation of an indigenous capacity in each country for research and development. But scientific careers have remarkably little prestige in many Southern countries. In such societies the more gifted individuals are recruited into fields other than in these devalued scientific careers. A number of them are doing research abroad, usually in Western countries. A major consideration in any national science policy has to be the establishment of the basic conditions and facilities to attract this reservoir of talent back to the region and retain those already there by more consideration and better salaries.

A last word should be said on the flight of capital which in some developing countries represents such an amount of money that it is almost equivalent to the totality of the external debt. Such a paradoxical situation should certainly be changed by governmental decisions and regulations.

The growing awareness of all these facts among the population will certainly play an essential role in pushing governments to give more attention to them, as has already been the case in some African, Asian and Latin American countries.

The Role of International Institutions In the past years, international financial institutions such as the World Bank, the European Economic Community and Japanese Official Development Aid have become aware of the problems of rural underdevelopment. The regional development Banks in Latin America, Africa and Asia, as well as those in the Middle East, should increasingly emphasize this type of operation. There is a new trend, as yet quite modest, of direct attribution of some financial means to small-scale projects without going through the governments. This increases the probability that the money will reach its destination without being diverted on the way, as was often the case in the past. But there is a certain structural incompatibility between large and bureaucratic administrations and small NGOs. The innovative enthusiasm of the latter as well as the daily urgency of their field work, leaves little time to deal with the bureaucratic requirements and administrative details expected of them.

To promote and accelerate this type of rural development, we think these institutions should devote a greater part of their budget to local initiatives and small-scale projects. This would strengthen their efficiency and assist their replication. They should also establish an advisory committee made up of Southern

NGOs and organisations such as the Club of Rome to extend their knowledge of the field, to guide their selection of propitious cases for financial support as well as to contribute to the evaluation of their results.

The most immediate responsibility of the international institutions, however, has to do with the debt problem in developing countries. And it is fitting to emphasize the positive evolution that has taken place in the last few years, which began with the agreement signed between the International Monetary Fund and Mexico in 1986, establishing a link, for the first time, between the level of growth of a country and the level of its debt payments. An evolution in thinking with regard to the debt problem today can be observed as much in the debtor countries as in the lender institutions.

In the debtor countries, the debt crisis has begun to induce a revision of development strategies and the implementation of policies aimed at reducing budgetary imbalances, fighting inflation, engaging in economic and financial recovery programmes and reconquering control over their economic policies. As for lender institutions, the International Monetary Fund in particular, the demand for necessary readjustment is now viewed with a higher awareness of the social consequences of overly brutal measures. It has become clearer that the debt problem can only be solved in the long term and only if—as is acknowledged by the plan once set forward by the then U.S. Secretary of Treasury James Baker—growth resumes both in the countries of the North and in the those of the South.

Very recently there appears to be a reorientation in

the thinking of the leaders of the international financial organisations.

For example, Enrique V. Iglesias,[6] discussing the transfer of real resources to developing countries, states:

> Among the areas of activity targeted by the Bank, a few stand out for the high priority they have been assigned, namely: the promotion of economic investments in key sectors of the economy such as energy, transport, communications, agricultural and industrial development; the alleviation of the social debt in the region (e.g., assistance to the low income segments of the population, cooperation for urban and agricultural development, promotion of small producers, enhancing women's participation in development); the support for the modernization of the private sector (e.g., loans and equity investments by the Inter-American Investment Corporation, and loans and technical cooperation from the Bank in the areas of trading systems modernization, export capacity development, financial sector modernization, cofinancing, and support to microentrepreneurs); the promotion of human resources development, particularly in the scientific and technological areas; and, finally, the promotion of environmental management and conservation of natural resources.

One valuable task for the Club of Rome is to convince policymakers of the notion that it is possible for

[6]President of the Inter-American Development Bank. September 24, 1990 at the joint Committee of the Boards of Governors of the Bank and the Fund on the transfer of real resources to developing countries.

North and South to work together so that development no longer demands such a high price of regional
and global environments. Development planning can
rely on already available advanced energy-efficient
and materials-efficient technologies. It can encourage
efforts to build up an endogenous system of scientific
and technological research capabilities in the developing countries. It must emphasize the use of local
resources and renewable energies to lead to a decen-
tralized and balanced pattern of development. At first
sight, the financial burden involved may seem too
onerous for developing countries. It need not be, if
aid-to-development policies can be designed to ensure
that adequate use is made of the advances achieved by
the technological revolution. Seen in a historical perspective, industrializing countries now have a great
advantage: they are building up their capital stock at
a time when new technological options are becoming
available. We have to ensure that these options do not
remain the privilege of the North, but can be ac-
cessed by the South on affordable terms. This would
be possible if, for example, a part of aid-to-development funds were to be used to give compensation to
the enterprises in the private sector for the outflow of
their technological know-how.

Moreover, we have to ask whether current conditions allow us to envisage successful international co-
operation on the necessary scale. Potentially, two
obstacles might bar the way. The first is political. Re-
laxation in tensions between East and West has
pointed to the emergence of a new international climate and this process may continue, despite worrying signs of an inversion in tendency within the
Soviet nomenclature. The new climate raises expecta-

tions in the context of East–West relations, but not necessarily of North–South. Indeed, confrontation between East and West often led to a competition in offering assistance to developing countries for political or trade advantages.

An attitude verging on impatience has become apparent among many economists and policymakers in the industrialized world of the North. They seem to feel that while restructuring the former Eastern bloc is a practical proposition, development of the South remains as intractable as ever. Furthermore, the Gulf War has given rise to increasing tension between North and South. The depth of fundamentalist feelings in the Islamic world threatens not only the objective analysis of economic interest, but also what has been a long tradition in much of the Arab world of tolerance for non-Muslim beliefs.

The Club of Rome can make its contribution. Top-down measures to find a policeable mechanism which can permit development to take place without unduly expanding total world resource use, and to condition market forces to take into account longer-term, hitherto unquantifiable parameters such as environmental quality and equity, are clearly required, but they will not be enough. They need to be flanked by an ethical mobilization worldwide if the challenge is to be overcome. Sacrifices are demanded of all people and the returns will only be seen by coming generations. Appeals to altruism are all very well: we need constant pressure for more education, greater awareness of the trade-offs between environment and growth, between development and a more equitable —and hence more secure—world order.

IMPACTS OF THE CHANGES AND IMPENDING CHANGES ON INDIVIDUALS AND SOCIETIES

The pressure of the facts is such that we must either change or disappear. To meet the three priorities that require immediate action and begin managing change without losing any time, a true transformation of mind-sets and behaviour is imperative.

The indispensable measures will be unpopular, costly and painful and wealth will inescapably have to be shared. This means a whole life-style and pattern of consumption will have to be modified in the industrialized countries, while in developing countries an entire mutation will have to take place to include a spirit of initiative, of discipline and higher standards on every level.

But minds are not in the least prepared for this multifaceted revolution. Unless public opinion is truly educated and intensely prepared for the acceptance of new living conditions, we can expect revolt and inertia to erupt just as governments and decision makers will be needing public support more than ever.

VIII

GOVERNANCE AND THE CAPACITY TO GOVERN

THE COMPLEX OF PROBLEMS THAT WE HAVE described leads to the question as to how they are to be mastered through policies that take full account of their mutual impacts. Are the traditional political, institutional and administrative systems capable of facing up to such a situation?

Knowing how to make the right decisions in full knowledge of the facts and then implementing them in time is no easy matter; yet it is a fundamental element of the problematique. The deficiencies of governance are at the root of many of the strands of the problematique and hence improved governance is an essential aspect of the resolutique.

In this chapter, we shall examine the origins of some of the problems of governance, its new dimensions and the adequacy of its present responses. We shall also make some suggestions as to changes which might contribute to the resolutique.

We use the term *governance* to denote the command-mechanism of a social system and its actions that endeavours to provide security, prosperity, coherence, order and continuity to the system. It necessarily embraces the ideology of the system, which may (democratic) or may not (authoritarian) define means for effective consideration of the public will and accountability of those in authority. It also includes the structure of government of the system, its policies and procedures. Some might say cynically that governance is the means to provide a stable equilibrium between the various centres of power. Taken broadly, the concept of governance should not be restricted to the national and international systems but should be used in relation to regional, provincial and local governments as well as to other social systems such as education and the military, to private enterprises and even to the microcosm of the family. It attempts to apply at least the semblance of rationality to the irrational, subjective and often contradictory behaviour of politicians, economists and the rest of us.

It is unwise to overgeneralize on governability; different countries have different approaches as well as different problems. Nevertheless, predominantly Western ideas have stimulated economic growth and material progress in a large part of the world and have brought with them Western structures and concepts, now generally accepted, although with many variations and diversely interpreted. The idea of governance is not new; its main core components go back at least 5,000 years and probably much longer.

We have already underscored the mismanagement of the world, evidence of which is all around us—oceans of misery and poverty, the arms trade, crippling indebtedness in the developing world, huge annual deficits in the United States with a national debt of some U.S. $3 trillion, rampant speculation, corruption and violence. Have we to conclude that the world is impossible to govern? Are our governors incompetent or ill-chosen? These are doubts which public opinion and citizens are raising—probably much more incisively than the politicians themselves. We have to ask ourselves three basic questions:

- Do we, at the end of this century, properly understand our world, or are our concepts and approaches no longer adapted to meet the complex and dangerous situation we face?

- Why, in spite of growing concern over several decades and innumerable international debates and many constructive proposals, have action and practical results been so limited?

- What suggestions can be made now to improve the effectiveness of the processes which should convert widespread concern into practical action?

The dangers of ineffective governance are present at three different levels; at the level of the individual and the family (which we have discussed under "The Human Malaise"), at the level of the national and of the level of international political systems.

New Dimensions of the Problem of Governance

Since the end of the Second World War the activities of governments have extended enormously. At the same time many of the areas under their jurisdiction demand highly specialized technical understanding.

We must therefore stress how much the complexity of national and international systems has grown. As André Danzin[1] puts it, "this sudden rise in complexity has thrown us out of a social system that was accessible to logic and thrust us into a social organisation dominated by cybernetic reactions." In a very complex environment with instabilities and imbalances, as is the situation of humankind today, the feedback systems are so numerous and so intertwined that it is difficult to design them within a comprehensive model. It is even less possible to grasp such systems through common sense and intuition or even to draw up an approximate mental image of them. The solution of problems within the complex system is therefore difficult, all the more so because in many cases public acceptance of solutions is unlikely to be achieved.

From what then, is this growth of complexity derived? We mention a few of the factors operating on both the national and the international levels:

- The increased speed of changes—technical, economic and demographic.

- The increase in the number of actors in the systems to be governed, whether a big city, a country, the vast areas of the South or humankind as a whole.

- The increase in the number of sovereign states playing an active role in any given international system.

- The intensity of interdependence between national societies over a wide range of matters such as transfer of

[1]Former general manager of Thomson CSF, member of the Club of Rome.

knowledge, periodic or permanent migratory flows, cultural influences and economic exchange.

▪ The coming into contact of heterogeneous societies, differing in their cultures, their values, their political traditions and their standard of living.

▪ The erosion of national sovereignty. In the words of Soedjatmoko[2]:

> In the process of interdependence, we have all become vulnerable. Our societies are permeable to decisions taken elsewhere in the world. The dynamics of interdependence might be better understood if we think of the globe not in terms of a map of nations but as a meteorological map, where weather systems swirl independently of any national boundaries and low and high fronts create new climatic conditions far ahead of them.

▪ The enormous volume of information, the speed of communication and the importance of the media as amplifier, selector, filter and distorter of what passes as information—despite the fact that in the South access to information is still very limited.

▪ The emergence of a new world technical system based on microelectronics.

[2]Former President of the United Nations University, former member of the Club of Rome (now deceased), Mr. Soedjakmoto wrote this statement in a paper contributed to the Club of Rome annual conference of 1985 held in Santander, Spain on the topic of "Governability of a World in Transition."

- The appearance of problems demanding management on a global scale of mankind's common heritage in areas such as climate, environment, the exploitation of the oceans and architectural heritage.

- The simultaneous consequences of technical development and the fragmentation of political power on the security of national societies.

- The dilemma of swollen bureaucracies. The nature and diversity of the problems to be solved and the systems (health, welfare, etc.) to be managed, encourage the growth of large bureaucracies which considerably increase resistance to change.

- In some national societies changing individual attitudes have led to increasing demands for services from the government. Citizens find it hard to believe that governments are unable to find solutions which will not cause them hardship or inconvenience. Simultaneously there is a decline in respect for authority and a lessening trust in and support for institutions.

Although far from exhaustive, this list suggests that most of these factors will be felt with increasing intensity in the twenty to thirty years to come. These new dimensions of governance place humankind in front of an entirely new historical situation. We must therefore not be surprised by the inadequacy of many of the answers currently given to the contemporary problems.

THE INADEQUACY OF THE RESPONSES TO CURRENT PROBLEMS

It is necessary to stress once more that the existence of tragic situations such as military conflict, threats to peace, violence of human rights, environmental damage and the intolerable persistance of widespread poverty and hunger in the world demonstrate the malfunction of the world system. Demographic, economic, political and environmental trends of global dimension, have combined in recent years to create a qualitatively distinct category of practical problems that were virtually unknown to traditional diplomacy. They are beyond the reach of individual national governments, cannot be fitted into accepted theories of competitive interstate behaviour and are coming increasingly to dominate world affairs. They cannot be wished away and they are indifferent to military intervention.

Inadequacies in the functioning of the system concern, above all, national governments and the intergovernmental international agencies. However, they also involve a wide range of other actors (individuals, political parties, firms, trade unions, educational systems, NGOs and so on) and the role they play or are not yet allowed to play in the operation of the world system.

The following are a few of the more obvious inadequacies displayed by national governments and intergovernmental bodies:

- While for some countries the principle of sovereignty is "the only basis for cohesion and national identity," it is increasingly incompatible with the realities of interdependence.

- Governments give priority to politically useful short-term solutions and systematically neglect the longer-term perspective. As a consequence of such legacies of neglect, problems tend to become compounded and governments fall into a rhythm of crisis government.

- Governments are organised mainly in the form of sectoral ministries, identify sectoral options, treat symptoms in isolation and propose static and local solutions. They are thus incapable as now organised to identify the problematique and apply the resolutique.

- In the allocation of resources between the many sectoral claimants, in many countries ministers with strong political power or strong personality find it easier to obtain credits than their weaker colleagues, thus creating imbalances.

- Central governments respond to challenges by attempting to increase their control over other agents thus generating random negative effects while generating demand for decentralization.

- When leaders make decisions in a situation of uncertainty, they suffer, not only from their inadequacies as human beings, but also from handicaps inherent to their role such as overwork, insufficient time for reflection, manipulated information, biased presentation of proposed decisions from lower positions in the hierarchy and often too great a reliance on subordinates.

- As for intergovernmental agencies, the system established immediately after the Second World War was rapidly designed to meet world needs as seen at the time. Henceforth, it grew "like Topsy," untidy and unplanned with additions to meet new needs as they were identified. Little thought was given to interactions and overlaps of the confusing mass of specialized units. As was inevitable, many of the agencies gradually began to cultivate their vested interests. Staff was recruited less on quality than on assuring, through quotas, an equitable distribution of posts to each member country. At the same time the effectiveness of some of the main agencies was diminished by overbureaucratization and politicization.

Attack on the complexity of the contemporary problems entails a double risk: that of excluding public opinion and elected representatives from the knowledge necessary for the understanding of a situation as well as that of strengthening the influence of specialists and experts whose arcane knowledge is difficult for the decision makers to appraise and check.

The complexity of the problems has been compounded by the number and complexity of the actors: political parties, trade unions, corporations, nongovernmental organisations as well as pressure groups of all kinds including informal groups which may be short-lived and nevertheless intense and effective in their mobilization on a particular issue. These various groups contribute to governance through their proposals and protests. *Governance is no longer the monopoly of governments and intergovernmental bodies and its effectiveness will depend on the capacity of leaders to selectively include in their decision making these new actors, which are in fact their partners in governance.*

THE STRUCTURES, POLICIES AND PROCEDURES OF GOVERNMENTS

Increasing obsolescence is thus a major characteristic of governance today. Its structures were in the essentials designed more than a century ago to meet the needs of much simpler societies than the present. Certainly some important innovations have taken place in the meantime such as the emergence of universal suffrage, the evolution of the welfare state and a recognition of human rights, but by and large change has been incremental or by extension of the already existing. It has been accompanied by high costs, swollen bureaucracies and inefficiency as the range of governmental intervention increased. Here we shall mention only a few of the areas where major innovations in structures and attitudes are most urgently required.

One such is the need for better mechanisms for the integration of sectoral policies as a consequence of the interactions of the problematique. In general government structures consist essentially of a series of vertical ministries for sectors such as agriculture, industry, education, health, defence and foreign affairs together with the central financial and economic mechanisms. This system has worked moderately well hitherto, but today many of the problem areas are "horizontal" and sprawl untidily across the whole vertical edifice of government. Hence elements of these issues tend to be tackled piecemeal, sector by sector.

National policy is often in practice the sum of a range of sectoral policies, not always harmonized, in the absence of overall integrating policies or mechanisms and the explicit statement of national objectives. In some countries, for example, urban problems are diffused over a dozen departments and agencies. Attainment of the goals of one department's policy may easily give rise to difficulties in other areas of policy or, at times, give rise to unexpected reinforcements. The complex, intertwined nature of contemporary problems suggests that, in the future, we must expect intersectoral conflicts more frequently that will delay decision making and implementation.

The integration of policy is, of course, the function of the president, the prime minister or the cabinet. In the fields of economic and foreign policies this is taken quite seriously in most countries. However, in other areas this is much less so. National leaders are so harassed by day-by-day pressing problems and putting out of political fires that they just do not have the time or the detailed information necessary to deal in depth with the extraordinarily wide range of interacting policies which contemporary government involves. The staff function, found so necessary by the military and by large corporations, is very weakly developed in most national administrations. Furthermore, when attempts are made to reinforce it by the introduction of advisors, this is often resented by the public as an inflation of the bureaucracy and by departmental ministers as a threat to their power and influence.

At lower levels of decision making the traditional approach to the harmonization of sectoral policies is the function of interdepartmental committees, useful certainly, but they can be a dreadful waste of time for senior line officials. It has to be admitted also that such committees are meeting points for representatives of various departmental vested interests, in tacit agreement not to rock the boat by questioning each others' policies and prerogatives. Incremental changes can be discussed openly, but ongoing policies and programmes are sacrosanct. In the final analysis, co-ordination is generally effected by the Treasury on financial grounds and often without concern for facts and objectives. The problems of horizontality became acute during the oil crisis of the 1970s when it was impossible to ignore the impact of shortage and price increase on a wide range of sectors from foreign policy to the environment. One solution was the creation of an Energy "Czar," expected to co-ordinate, but given no real powers to do so. Another was to create super ministries by coalescence of some of the existing agencies, but experience showed that the barriers between sections of a department could be as impenetrable as those between the former separate ministries.

A second area of difficulty concerns the conflict between long and short-term issues. This is a major and endemic problem. The normal parliamentary cycle of four or five years between elections is a feature of democratic governance. The power game of party politics determines that both administrations and oppositions have to respond quickly to issues which are of immediate concern to the electorate, if they are to retain or to achieve power at the next election.

Governments, like individuals, tend to ignore problems that can be put off till tomorrow—in this case until after the next election. This has probably mattered little in the past, but in periods of rapid change such as the present, what formerly appeared as long-term tends to race into the period just five to ten years ahead (i.e., into the period of the next administration). As a consequence, the new government inherits a legacy of neglect; untackled problems come home to roost, become compounded and there is descent to a rhythm of crisis government, a staggering from one emergency to the next—monetary, social, balance of payments, unemployment, inflation and the rest. Each crisis is resolved by pasting paper over the cracks, remedial measures seldom reach the roots of the difficulty. Fundamental causes of the difficulties, being long-term in their operation, are too easily ignored or unidentified in favour of cosmetic measures of ephemeral importance.

A further critical area is that of the appropriate levels of decision making. The current situation is somewhat of a paradox. The complexity and highly technical nature of problems encourages centralization for their analysis and solution which it would be difficult for regional and provincial bodies to replicate. Also the global coverage of so many of the problems demanding attention on the world scale would seem to require centralized national decisions. At the same time there is an increasing clamour for decentralization, regional autonomy and greater participation of the individual citizen in decisions which affect him closely. This tendency is being strongly reinforced at present by demands for independence or autonomy of innumerable ethnic groups as illustrated by the situation in Yugoslavia and the incredible fractionalization tendencies in the Soviet Union.

These two approaches are indeed two sides of the same coin, perhaps growing pains in the transition of the nation-state towards some new kind of global system. In the medium terms, the essential issue is how to establish, in a manner aiming at harmonious governance, a system in which there will be several layers of decision making, in which the basic principle will be to ensure that debate takes place and decisions are made as near as possible to those who will enjoy or suffer the results. For the global problems we need a global forum and, at the other extreme, local matters call for the town or community meeting rather than interpretation of edicts emanating from a remote and seemingly uncaring central government.

Finally, a few words about the bureaucracy. In many countries there is general public criticism of the size and power of the bureaucracy which seems to enjoy inventing petty restrictions to freedom and to unnecessarily complicate the life of citizens. It is felt to be remote, unresponsive and unfeeling, made up of people with tenured jobs who revel in their petty corners of power. No matter how intelligent and objective the Civil Service may be—and in many countries this is uncontroversial—it is realized that its members are selected to provide stability and continuity as political administrations come and go. Hence they are seen to stand for the status quo, to be the apotheosis of inertia and resistance to change, especially radical change. In some instances it is felt that the faceless Civil Service is out of the control of its political masters and thus not accountable to the people. Certainly, it is extremely difficult for a minister to master all the details of his departmental activities of which he has probably had no prior experience, while his officials, highly and professionally informed, "know all the answers."

There is undoubtedly some reality in these criticisms and equally at times a good deal of benefit in the informed caution of the official when faced with an inexperienced minister. The considerable extension of government responsibility in recent years into so many aspects of life has inevitably led to bureaucratic inflation and in some instances, such as defence, to perpetuation of power and policies. Internal policies may at times be creating dangerous and partly concealed vested interests.

SOME PARTICULAR ISSUES

Having outlined some general considerations on governance, we feel it necessary to discuss some aspects in more detail.

Resistance to Change   Governments seldom generate innovation. They react to pressures for change which arise from popular demands, either through the democratic process of elections or in the aftermath of a successful revolution. However, in reacting to demands for new approaches the natural conservatism of administrations (and not only its civil service component) is often able to put on the brakes. Their approaches are essentially linear and are based on either rigid rules of procedure and behaviour, or else on accumulated case experience. Like other institutions they are not given to self-criticism and, when subject to pressures outside, react defensively. They feel that their methods have been rendered optimal by experience and that they are the only reasonable means of solving problems. Suggestions for improvement are shrugged off—"We tried that years ago and it didn't work." It is rare that mistakes are admitted, or missed opportunities recognized. Problems are treated in a sequential order and mistakes resulting from slightly wrong decisions with regard to slightly misunderstood challenges accumulate. In a benevolent environment such as that which existed during the long period of economic growth, warning signals are few and dangers seem too far off to keep the organisations alert, rather than resting on their laurels. Now the environment appears to have become hostile and the expedients of the past no longer seem to work.

With the uncertainties inherent in the global revolution, such approaches will have to be abandoned and the need is for institutions which are flexible and dynamic, often provisional or deliberately temporary. The objective of stability will have to be replaced by one of resilience to meet fast moving needs and opportunities. There will have to be a much greater degree of transparency and less distinction between the strictly official and the unofficial. All this will require a change in the psychology of both officials and politicians with the entry into the system, for longer or shorter periods, of individuals from industries, trade unions, academia, etc. Here as elsewhere in our society of change, education and training will be of great importance. It is difficult to teach old dogs new tricks, and serious and lengthy recycling will be needed for both officials and politicians.

Corruption Political and moral corruption are rampant in many countries and are growing. Their eradication is essential as a prerequisite to the development of effective and just government. How to do this is difficult. Certainly, mere exortation is useless, while revolution often leads merely to a worsening of the situation and simple change of patronage. This problem demands deep consideration, but undoubtedly a considerable increase of transparency in governance is the first step.

Confrontation Versus Consensus   In most of the democratic countries operating on a multiparty system, a model of confrontation has evolved and spread throughout national life. In moderation this can be a healthy situation. The so-called concept of creative friction of management–labour relations had a justification in the continuous improvement of the condition of the workers, while in politics it has done a good deal to prevent excessive complacency and stagnation. However, it has gone too far and we see many examples of party interests being placed above the national good. While in no way arguing against party politics as such, there are strong reasons for attempting, in both political and industrial relations, to inculcate a change of attitude in the direction of consensus-building. In face of the gravity of the decisions that will have to be taken in the near future, artificially stimulated party rivalries, generated by attempts to win popular votes at the next election and often not even based on real ideological differences, could lead to disaster. There is an overwhelming need to establish the maximum of common agreement between political parties claiming to be custodians of the national good, if we are to weather the many storms ahead. To this end it would be useful to bring together representatives of different parties in a nonpolitical forum such as might be provided by the

Club of Rome and similar bodies, for the discussion of specific issues.

Government and the Forces of the Market   In Eastern Europe, abandonment of state-planned economies towards democracy has inevitably made clear the need for economic efficiency based on competition and incentive (i.e., to accept and operate the forces of the market). Acceptance of this has led to a wide-spread euphoria which assumes that this is their panacea. While fully in favour of the need for these countries to operate on the basis of the market forces, we have already warned of the danger of relying exclusively on them. Here it is necessary to discuss briefly the relationship between governments and the markets.

The market is ill-adapted to deal with long-term effects, intergenerational responsibilities and common property resources. It operates essentially to short-term signals and thus its indications can be gravely misleading if applied to long-term needs. The system of the market economy countries based on competition is motivated by self-interest and ultimately on greed. In the absence of all restraints, brutal operation of the market forces would lead to exploitation, neglect of social needs, environmental destruction and the short-term consumption of resources essential for the future. However, society demands and industry and commerce accept that there has to be an agreed-upon system of ethics, within which the market is operated; the system is thus self-regulating to some extent.

The market system has flaws, certainly. Nevertheless, competition and incentive are undoubtedly effective, in the current allocation of resources, in developing new technologies and in the generation of the material prosperity which the industrialized countries enjoy today.

Even those governments most devoted to the concepts of private enterprise recognize the need to define the boundaries within which the market can function. In the general public interest, governments have to provide a firm framework of regulations for the private sector and to establish mechanisms for the correction of abuses effectively. At the same time governmental policies are necessary for the establishment of an economic climate propitious for the efficient functioning of the market within the country and to ensure that its products are competitive on the international market. Government strategies should also provide incentives for longer-term development, for example, by fiscal and other incentives to encourage industry to invest in scientific research and technological development towards longer-term sustainability. Japan has been particularly successful in developing a system combining business initiative and government incentive. Close collaboration between the public and the private sectors has been established as a basis for long-term technological development, particularly through publicly financed research programmes, with wide participation of private enterprise.

It is particularly important, at the moment, that those countries which are now moving vigorously from centrally planned to market-oriented economies, should recognize the limitations as well as the benefits of the market.

Humanity in Politics There is need to introduce a new strain of humanity into politics. Recent years have seen a marked loss of confidence in political parties and personalities, contempt for bureaucracy, voter abstention and a general alienation from the establishment and society. This may be due partly to overcentralization, which depersonalizes the system, and to bureaucratic oppression. It is a symptom of deep malaise. Leaders and bureaucrats seem to have forgotten that politics (like economics) is about people and serves people. Until humanity and compassion permeate politics and go beyond baby-kissing during election campaigns, alienation will persist.

THE INTERNATIONAL DIMENSION

We have already touched upon several difficulties of international governance, where many of the problems of the national level are compounded. The trend towards globality and recognition that many of the contemporary problems are essentially global and cannot be solved through individual country initiatives gives a greatly enhanced importance to the United Nations and other international systems. Furthermore, recent events suggest that the nations may at last be willing to give the United Nations a considerably bigger role in the peacekeeping process and in environmental survival.

The United Nations System as initially conceived and with the multitude of agencies and programmes which were subsequently added in haphazard growth is no longer what the world in global revolution requires. The need for reform has long been recognized, but it has not been possible to achieve owing to the long geopolitical stalemate. This has now changed. The Soviet Union is taking an active approach in UN matters and United States' reticence appears to be diminishing. The time seems ripe, therefore, for a complete overhaul of the system, using, in addition to new analyses, the innumerable studies of UN reform needs which have been made during the last decade. We strongly urge, therefore, that an immediate start be made to redesign the system and that the process not be left entirely to representatives of the various ministries of foreign affairs. Experts from industry and academia have many important contributions to make.

Part of the review would aim at the reexamination of the mandates and activities of the multitude of agencies and programmes, with a view to harmonizing their mandates, sharpening their focus and ensuring a relatively balanced coverage of the vast range of interests. At present there is the appearance of a good deal of duplication among these bodies. Much of this is desirable in terms of the problematique. A subject such as technology finds itself in UNESCO, as arising from the science element of the UNESCO mandate. It is also centred in UNIDO[3] in the industrial development context, while UNEP[4] has to examine its consequences. Again concern for technology is inevitable in ILO,[5] FAO, UNDP and

[3]United Nations Industrial Development Organisation.
[4]United Nations Environment Programme.
[5]International Labour Organisation.

the World Bank. In many areas there is nevertheless great need for coordination between agencies. There exist, of course, the obvious interagency committees, but institutional rivalries produce the same kind of ineffectiveness that we have described in the case of interdepartmental committees on the national level.

The importance and nature of many of the global problems suggests that new and flexible ways must be sought to tackle such issues which, in their complexity, fit uneasily within the programmes of particular agencies or institutions. In a more coherent UN system it should be possible to designate certain problem areas as necessitating a combined approach from several of the specialized bodies. Programmes would then be set up in which the participating agencies would take part in terms of both finance and expertise, with some support from the centre where appropriate. Such a scheme would entail more influence of the UN centre in the work of the specialist bodies, but this might not be a bad thing if it could be done with minimum bureaucratic interference and if the programmes were genuinely autonomous.

New approaches are also needed in the normal working of some of the individual agencies. Intergovernmental organisations, just as governmental agencies on the national scale, are not propitious locations for the conduct of research. They can stimulate, formulate problems and provide for useful international discussions, but lack of sufficient funds prevents them from undertaking research in depth. Their work is essentially catalytic.

The vast number of topics which an organisation such as UNESCO has to examine makes it impossible to have a competent staff, expert in all the detailed subjects covered. Furthermore, areas of particular concern necessarily change, so that many matters of focus are only temporary on the agenda, with the new points of attack requiring a quite different set of skills. This problem is dealt with in most agencies by the use of consultants, but it would seem more efficient to adopt policies of delegating responsibility for particular studies to the most competent institutes in the world for each subject undertaken. Selection of competent individuals should be essentially on the basis of quality and there should be no question of applying the principle of the "juste retour." With such a system, the headquarters staff of high-quality individuals with a wide breadth of interests and contacts could be kept quite small.

Finally, we must mention the question of leadership and especially the high qualities looked for in the person of the Secretary General. This subject has been usefully discussed in a recent report of the Dag Hammarskjold Foundation. The UN Charter described the holder as essentially the chief administrative officer of the Organisation, but it soon became obvious that important political mediating and leadership functions were inevitable. In the reformed and active United Nations of the future, the image of the Secretary General is vitally important. For millions of people throughout the world he personalizes what would otherwise be seen as yet another vast bureaucratic machine. The qualities desired in this individual are almost superhumanly demanding; he or she (there has never yet been a feminine candidate) must be brave and at the same time cautious, must have an outstanding grasp of the world situation and problems, have a high degree of objectivity and be able to project an image of impartiality, be highly intelligent and diplomatic, be innovative and appear as a great world leader. Not least, the rigour of the function is such that an enormous physical stamina is demanded.

The process of finding and appointing a Secretary General appears to be a curiously haphazard hit-and-miss affair which takes place under the shadow of the veto. Candidates emerge unsystematically, either self-promoted or suggested by governments. It is an essentially in-house affair, names being discussed in corridors and in innumerable meeting rooms and in practice the final decision is taken by the five permanent members of the Security Council and endorsed by the General Assembly. There are many wise people of stature outside diplomatic and government circles who possess the necessary qualities and, with every respect to the present incumbent, we suggest that for the future a more open and systematic selection method should be devised in order to find the "best man for the job."

THE CAPACITY TO GOVERN

This leads to a general reappraisal of the qualities which are called for in those we select to govern us. Reform of structures, procedures and attitudes will be of little avail unless men and women of the right quality and capacity are willing to serve and the citizens capable of appreciating these qualities are willing to vote for them. It is simply not good enough that access to leadership be achieved through good television performances and simplistic speeches aimed at manipulating the masses into enthusiastic support with empty promises and avoidance of realities. There can be no generalized "identikit" for the appropriate qualities in view of the diversity of situations and cultures; however, against the need for leaders with a new profile for a new world, we note some indication of the qualities to be sought:

- a strategic vision and a global approach to the priority elements of the problematique;

- a capacity for innovation and adjustment to change;

- an ethical perspective, making no concessions to expediency;

- effectiveness in taking decisions after due dialogue with colleagues and advisers, in ensuring the implementation of the decisions and, in due time, in assessing the results;

- capacity to learn and to encourage others to learn;

- courage to change his or her mind as perceptions of situations and problems deepen; in today's confrontational climate this can at times be political suicide;

- ability to inform the public clearly of the general direction of policy in a way which encourages them to identify;

- capacity to relegate strategy and tactics to their proper place as means and not as ends;

- willingness to set up systems through which he can listen in to the needs of the citizens, their fears, demands and suggestions.

These then are some of the desiderata; what about the present realities? At present, even in those countries where corruption in government is not rampant, the rewards of leadership, while in theory those of serving society and the satisfaction of doing a good job are, in practice, all too often enjoyment of power. Hence, those who present themselves for election, tend to be individuals with more than the average of vanity and the urge for power over others. These are hardly the criteria for the selection of the wisest people to guide the world through the difficulties of the revolution. As things are now, many people of high quality who are potentially national or world leaders avoid entering the political arena with all its vulgarity and backbiting and the paucity of its awards for those for whom power is not the primary consideration.

Much attention is therefore required with regard to the selection of our leaders. At present, this is done by a survival of the fittest process which tends to select persons who are overtly self-seeking and at times willing even to sacrifice the common good for their personal or party ambitions. The qualities which are essential for the attainment of high office are thus frequently the very attributes which make the individual unfit for it. Charisma is an extremely important asset for a leader, but it is not sufficient and it is very often associated with other less desirable qualities. Yet, thanks to television, charisma is probably the most important ingredient in gaining election. It is difficult to see how this can be changed; it will certainly not happen from within the system and there is therefore a need for wise individuals without political ambition to expose these problems to the public.

Political decisions are seldom based on rationality. They are normally made, in each individual case, on a complex mixture of intuition, usefully drawn from experience, personal motivations, often unconscious, constraints of political dogma and expediency. This is unlikely to change, but the process can be educated; much better and more thoroughly analysed information can be made available, motivations can be more consciously recognized and thus modified and expediency can be replaced if the system permits longer-term considerations.

In the changing circumstances which we have assumed throughout, it is essential that forward-looking governments at all levels develop an extent of policy entrepreneurship and not merely attempt to maintain stability and harmony amid the whirl of confusing events. It is necessary that the ship of state be not only kept afloat, but that it should be steered, surely and deliberately, toward a desired destination. Thus, future governments must learn to become, to a degree, social architects. For this purpose, a much deeper and continuing discussion of issues is required within the framework of national and world trends. The staff function becomes ever more important and the whole art and science of policy advice comes into question. Policy advisers should not consist wholly or mainly of officials, but should include individuals from many disciplines and without party political affiliation. The whole question of policy analysts is an open book and much thought needs to be given as to how this aspect of the staff function can be utilized.

IX

AGENTS OF THE RESOLUTIQUE

THE PRIMARY AGENTS OF THE RESOLUTIQUE are those that will allow individuals and societies to learn how to adapt to the changes that are constantly modifying the face of the planet.

Adjustment to change is the fundamental challenge that we find underlying all the constituent elements of the problematique analysed in the first part of this book, a challenge addressed to all the people of our planet, whatever their culture, traditions, religion or philosophical option, whatever their training.

Any change, for better or for worse, implies learning, self-examination, one's relationship to others and to the environment. Such questioning demands effort and will inevitably be difficult. Having been brought up to stand firmly in their certitudes—values, profession, faith, etc.—human beings are now facing not one change, but an uninterrupted chain of changes that affect the very orientation of their entire existence. To make things more difficult, changes are succeeding one another with unprecedented speed. The challenge is therefore not to adapt once and for all to a new situation, but to get into a permanent state of adaptation in order to be able to face uncertainty, the new dimensions of complexity and the insidious or brutal changes and potential opportunities affecting our world as a whole and human beings in their immediate environment.

A mutant situation such as this does not mean that the human being should passively allow himself to be modeled by the changes and suffer them without reaction. Neither does it imply that he must live under permanent stress for not knowing how to understand or overcome the unprecedented phenomena.

What instruments can he use to understand the changes and safeguard his freedom and discernment capability? How can he become, not an isolated spectator wallowing in his own pessimism but an actor organised and capable of contributing through his spirit of innovation and his willpower to the building of the society he deeply desires.

Among the agents of the resolutique, the individual has three at his disposal to go through this transitional period. There is nothing very new about them, but the resolutique approach gives them the proper dimensions to meet the new perspective. They are: the learning challenge of education, the contribution of science and the new technologies and the role of mass media.

In all of the preceding chapters, we have used different terms to refer to the same imperative: to learn, to understand, to communicate, to inform, to adapt, to manage. These words have rung insistently throughout because in fact the problem of education constantly appears as a leitmotiv—learning in and from life and not just what is taught in school, understanding the world in mutation in which we live, adjusting to new technologies, engaging in interdisciplinary communication on the planetary dimension into which we have been projected, acting out of responsibility: education is all this, even if the term may seem worn from overuse. Indeed, the educational systems of most countries are undergoing a crisis and seldom fill existing needs. We have today to define other objectives and other priorities. We are evermore aware that the educational systems, the schools, the universities are only ensuring part of what we call education, and that the family, the professional framework and many other social cells are, on various levels, playing the role of education. The crisis in education makes it an essential element of the world problematique, but it is increasingly appearing also as a privileged agent of the resolutique. This is why it constitutes a prime articulation in the problematique–resolutique pair.

1. The Learning Challenge

First of all, we have to repeat that to our mind, the term *education* goes far beyond the existing school systems. We see the most important task of education *as learning how to learn.*[1] It may be a truism to say that education is the key to the quality of human resources. But this is only so if education is understood as a series of processes that not only shape *vocational*

---

[1] See *No Limits to Learning*, report to the Club of Rome, (Botkin, Elmandjra, Malitza, 1978).

qualifications, but also enable the individual to actualize his or her potentiality by absorbing and mastering the cultural factors necessary for intelligent participation in society, the acceptance of responsibility and the existence of true human dignity.

Unfortunately, knowledge and social relations have reached such a state of complexity that the educational system has become a natural prey to three afflictions—plethora of knowledge, anachronism and unsuitability.

This *plethora of knowledge* applies at all age levels. The sheer scale of the accumulation of knowledge in all fields means that we no longer know how to select what should be transmitted to children and students. To take an example, the quantity of scientific and technical publications in 1986 alone equalled and perhaps surpassed the production of all scholars and experts from the remotest past up to the Second World War. How is such a flood of information to be sorted out? How is it to be transmitted? How can we select what is to be transmitted?

Anachronism comes about because this flood of information is constantly being renewed: ideas are modified as new knowledge extends and qualifies the old. Yet practically nowhere are primary and secondary teachers retrained. They teach what they were taught twenty years before in quite a different environment. Even with retraining—which would be an immense progress in itself—they would still be behind the times since it is not possible to pass on knowledge until it has matured and been digested, and this process takes time.

Unsuitability is what children and young people confusedly feel to be characteristic of the conventional education they receive, since it does not properly relate to the world they have to face. Television and strip cartoon, novels and science-fiction films, the universe of concrete, glass and aluminium, all seem a far cry from what is taught at school. All too often vocational training does not prepare them for the true needs of the labour market and sometimes even trains them for jobs that no longer exist. This situation is difficult to remedy, since the effects of structural and curriculum reform—with all their unwanted side-effects—are felt only in the long term —after at least ten or fifteen years. But that long term cannot be predicted.

If education has been traditionally considered a function of teaching, today and even more in the future education means the permanent process of learning by every human being in society. Learning change has become one of the new prior objectives of education.

> "Listen, look, understand, for thus it is on earth. Do not be idle, do not walk aimlessly, do not wander without a destination. How should you live? How should you go on for a short time? They say it is very difficult to live on the earth, a place of terrific struggle, my little lady, my little bird, my little one."
>
> Huethuetlatolli
> Pre-Columbian teaching

From their very infancy, human beings begin to learn by acting, participating and experimenting, and not merely looking on passively. Even in early childhood, a human being is learning to be a protagonist rather than a spectator. It is in this active relationship with his human, natural and physical environment, and solely in this relationship, that a person's freedom, independence, personality and creativity will develop and reach their full level of development. It should be remembered, though, that to act positively does not imply the abolition of all rules or the rejection of restrictions.

The education of every human being at any age must embrace multiple functions that mark out the learning process and guide it towards the immediate future, with the following objectives:

- acquiring knowledge;

- structuring intelligence and developing the critical faculties;

- developing self-knowledge and awareness of one's gifts and limitations;

- learning to overcome undesirable impulses and destructive behaviour;

- permanently awakening each person's creative and imaginative faculties;

- learning to play a responsible role in the life of society;

- learning to communicate with others;

- helping people to adapt to and prepare for change;

- enabling each person to acquire a global view of the world;

• training people to become operational and capable of problem-solving.

In the world of today, these last four points constitute the only way to prepare future adults to face the world of tomorrow, but they are still practically ignored in the classic educational processes. All kinds of more or less convincing reasons are invoked to explain this—from the overloaded curricula to the inadequate training of the teachers in quasi-unexplored fields. Some countries, such as France, introduce as compulsory a school subject which they call Civic Education. It seems obvious that "World Education," as a subject, or better yet "Introduction to the Great World Problems and the Problematique" should henceforth be a compulsory subject in the education of children and adolescents.

The role of the teacher to whom the future of the child is entrusted is one of the most noble of society and requires dedication and a sense of vocation. Yet in many places the teacher is undervalued, underpaid and given a relatively low status in society. The need to recruit minds and motivations of the highest quality into this profession demands a new social attitude on the part of the public and especially of parents. This profession, on which the future depends, must be given status and reward that will attract the best and its training colleges will have to be elevated so as to provide not only the highest quality of instruction and stimulation but the inculcation of prospective and participative attitudes. This is one of the key issues of educational reform because of the multiplying influence which it would exert.

Education should consciously and decisively involve the individual in a permanent, life-long process beginning in the home and family, continuing in the appropriate scholastic setting and then in the work-place, in leisure activities, in the religious environ-ment as well as in the community or in other organised groups such as trade unions or in political life, and extending right through the retirement years in personal and altruistic pursuits.

Education should also meet the need for a multidis-ciplinary approach, for each problem has many ele-ments, technical, economic, social, political and human and can seldom be resolved by the politician, scientist, engineer or economist in isolation. With the increasing interdependence of nations and the emer-gence of so many problems of global dimension, many disciplines have to be called simultaneously into play. Yet multidisciplinary action is difficult to achieve, for society is organised essentially on a verti-cal basis. Government departments are grouped by sector, and the policies of each are devised with only secondary consideration of their effects on the poli-cies of the others. The same may be said of the uni-versities, organised into faculty, departmental and subdepartmental, each pursuing a deeper under-standing of its particular specialization and usually unfamiliar with the findings of other sections.

Experience shows that when specialists from dif-ferent disciplines are identified as a team with the solution of a common, complex problem, they are able to establish communication allowing each to ap-ply the insights of his subject to the problem. How-ever, all the incentives present in academia work against such an approach, for reputation and pro-motion depend on the judgment of peers who as successful *specialists* give little credit to contributions from the multidisciplinary team and, indeed, are inclined to dismiss such work as a diversion or dilettantism.

The men and women of today and tomorrow who have been brought up to stand on certitudes must and shall increasingly have to observe the evolution of the world that surrounds them, to live in a world of complexity and uncertainty. Hence they need to develop their own capacities for innovation, adjustment to change and the management of instability such as to make it creative.[2] For their spiritual and intellectual balance, for their ability to overcome so-called stress situations, they need new arms which they can actually find within themselves, though they are not aware of them and have never practiced using them. They will have to resort to combinations that have been scorned for too long: "the human being is a thinking reed," wrote Pascal. But that which is cerebral and intellectual in him cannot approach so mysterious a truth as reality unless it equally resorts to the apparently irrational, the intuitive and the emotional, which are, to a great extent, the foundation of human relationships.

The role of education is even more vital than we have imagined. But it will take much research and work to rethink the concept of education and enable it to open up to the dimensions of the coming times such that the educators of today and tomorrow will be in a better position to discover the immensity and the nobility of their task: to lead the way to an evolu-

[2]Ilya Prigogine, Nobel Physics laureate and member of the Club of Rome, develops this topic brilliantly in his works.

tion of the mind and behaviour and thus to give birth to the new—one and manifold—civilization.

2. The Contribution of Science and Technology

In the industrialized countries of the North, society has been shaped by technology, the way of life has adapted to make full use of it and prosperity has been built on it. Technology imported from the industrialized world has also penetrated into the urbanized areas of the South. At the same time, many of the problems of contemporary society have been caused directly or indirectly by technology or more often by its misuse. It is to be expected, therefore, that technology with its seminal partner science will be an essential element of the resolutique.

Science and technology are too often loosely assumed to be more or less two aspects of the same thing—Research and Development gives rise to Science and Technology. In reality, the system of science and that of technology are very different. That of science is open and its product is freely disseminated through the world; that of technology is directed by economic motivations and its products are jealously guarded commercial property.

The role of science is to uncover knowledge. Its process explores the unknown and provides new data. Data is not itself information but the raw material of information, through selection with a sense of relevance, human intelligence orders and coalesces data to produce information. A matrix of information can become knowledge. Again knowledge does not spontaneously generate understanding; this requires for its arising, wisdom born of experience. Thus we are concerned with a continuum which runs from crude data, through information and knowledge to the end refinement of wisdom. Data we possess in large quantities and information can easily be concealed and lost in its disorder. Today we have enormously greater amounts of information and knowledge about man and the universe than our forefathers had, but there are few signs that human wisdom has increased significantly over the last 5,000 years. In these difficult and complex times we begin to realize that the pursuit of wisdom is the essential challenge that faces humanity.

> "Where is the knowledge which is lost in information?
>
> And where is the wisdom that is lost in knowledge?"
>
> T. S. Eliot

One would expect, therefore, that research on the nature of wisdom and its generation would be a number one priority. But have we the ingredients to start such a project and if presented to one of the great foundations, would it have a hope of acceptance? However, in recent years much knowledge has been gained on the workings of the brain, on brain and human behaviour and indeed on the nature of homo sapiens. Such interdisciplinary research, which involves biochemistry, physiology, neurology, endocrinology, molecular biology, psychology, anthropology and many other sciences, holds great promise and should be actively supported although its findings may seem, at this stage, merely theoretical. It should explore not only the rational mind but also emotional and intuitional aspects of being which play such an important part in the life of the individual and his often apparently irrational attitudes and behaviour.

Research aimed at the extension of knowledge without any aim of immediate practical use is known as *pure* or *fundamental research* and its scientific product is an element in the mosaic of ever-growing knowledge. It is usually undertaken in the university laboratories or, as in the Eastern European countries, in the Institutes of Academies of Science. *Scientific understanding,* arising from pure research, is an essential element of contemporary culture. *University research* also has an important educational function. University teachers who are actively engaged in research and hence working at the advancing frontiers of knowledge are able to transmit the spirit of the scientific method and to inspire their students. This function is as important in the less-developed as in the industrialized countries. Indeed it is a prerequisite to the understanding of today's world, necessary if the offerings of science and technology are to be usefully included in the process of development.

There is a second type of fundamental research increasingly pursued in industrialized regions, namely *oriented fundamental research,* which is an essential feature of input in the development of the most advanced technologies. Such research, while not expected to have direct practical application, is needed to illuminate areas of ignorance which have to be overcome in the development of advanced technical processes. Such research may be carried out in the laboratories of corporations or under contract by universities. It can thus be a very useful link between industry and academia.

Much research today is of a directly applied nature, aimed at solving specific problems in industry, agriculture or the public services. It may, by nature, be research in the natural sciences such as chemistry, physics and biology or in economics and the behavioural sciences. Indeed, the complexity of so many of the contemporary problems demands a combined attack from several disciplines. Experience shows that in such multidisciplinary approaches, research workers from many sciences, natural and social, in dealing with a particular complex problem, soon acquire a degree of communication which transcends the boundaries between the disciplines. The cultivation of multidisciplinary research is urgently required by the resolutique. It is difficult to generate within the universities, which are vertically organised into departments and faculties often with little contact. Applied research of course needs to be greatly extended in the developing countries where it is already widely if insufficiently pursued in the agricultural sector. In such countries it is much less common in industry, since the small size and relatively low level of sophistication of firms makes it difficult to identify technical problems or to afford to employ scientists to solve them.

Technological development is the essential, but only the initial step in industrial innovation. It consists in bringing together technical knowledge acquired through research or by purchase and to evolve it through the chemical pilot plant or engineering prototype so as to be a reliable and effective manufacturing process, competitive on the market. The cost of the development phase is usually an order of magnitude more expensive than the research stage on which it is based. But there are many other elements in technological innovation such as market surveys to test out the potential demand for the new product and hence its economic viability, the acquisition of risk capital and of management skills as well as recruitment and training of a reliable work force. The cost and complexity of industrial innovation has meant that much of the industrialization in developing countries has been done by the multinationals or by the import of turnkey technologies from abroad. Technological transfer has often proved to be a failure, either because of insufficient experience in the importing country in the selection of technologies appropriate to its needs and traditions, lack of negotiating skill or absence of sufficient technological and managerial experience. The newly industrialized countries of South East Asia have succeeded in their development, by following the postwar path of Japan in concentrating initially on building up the educational system, establishing modern research and development Institutes and then importing carefully selected processes. The larger developing countries also have already built up a sufficient capacity in science and technology so as to be able to select with confidence technologies from abroad, tailored to their needs, and to undertake original innovation.

The challenges thrown up by the turbulance of the global revolution indicate the need for a substantial reorientation of research and development programmes and a radical reordering of priorities. This is not the place to put forward detailed proposals, even should we be capable of doing so. Nevertheless it may be useful to suggest some broad lines of approach.

Fundamental Research   As argued above, effort should be put into investigations concerning the human individual, his nature, motivations, potentialities and limitations as well as into the social, educational and other structures which project human qualities and defects. There should be encouragement of fundamental research in the developing countries and the provision of adequate facilities for the upgrading of the knowledge of scientists from the South such as those of Abdus Salam's[3] International Centre for Theoretical Physics in Trieste.

Research on the Operation of the Natural System of the Planet   We know all too little about the tolerances of the system and of its reactions to human impacts. Sophisticated models of the global climate system have shown its extreme complexity and the need for still more detailed knowledge concerning regional and local impacts of human activity, greatly necessary if we are to foresee the consequences of earth-warming and the other macropollutions. There are great gaps of knowledge, for instance concerning the sinks for carbon dioxide; it is said that only between a third and a half of the emitted gas can be accounted for. There are vast zones of ignorance which must be closed if we are to learn sufficiently about the tolerance of the system before we destroy it and ourselves—through ignorance.

[3]Nobel laureate in physics, member of the Club of Rome.

Research Leading to Technological Innovations Such research, aimed at solving or alleviating many contemporary problems, will be both remedial and preventive. We shall outline here a few of the most obvious lines of attack.

As already stressed, there is an immediate need for a massive campaign on energy conservation and efficiency. On the conservation side, the requirement is more for the application of well understood techniques than for research. However, to be successful there will have to be considerable changes in human habits and this will entail new activities of the social sciences. There is, however, great scope for research aimed at improving efficiency in the generation, transmission and utilization of energy, for example, by the use of superconductivity, in the design of new types of engines, in machines of a wide variety of types and in chemical manufacture. Techniques of energy accounting need to be developed and applied. While the bulk of these efforts will have to be made in the countries of the North with their energy-intensive economies, the South with its increasing populations will face the same needs. It is encouraging to note the recognition of this in the recent Nairobi Declaration on Climatic Change (May 1990).

Second, it will be necessary to give a very high priority to an international programme of research for alternative energy sources and for corresponding work in the individual countries. This should include nuclear fusion development, magnetohydrodynamics and the whole range of soft energies. Work should also be accelerated on the possibilities of a future hydrogen economy, the gas being produced by the decomposition of water by electrolytic or catalytic means. This is not an alternative energy but an energy transmission method for use as a fuel in automobiles, aircraft, etc., if oil becomes costly or is discouraged for earth-warming reasons.

Beyond this, a search must be made for new, clean technologies and for the cleaning up of traditional processes. In the chemical industry, for example, research might be directed towards finding more specific synthetic routes including research on new catalysts. In this industry research must also be aimed at making toxic wastes harmless and doing so with minimum energy expenditure. Here, as in other industries, research on recycling techniques is required. A further task for the chemical industry is to devise biodegradable plastics for packaging and other purposes.

In agriculture and the agroindustries a determined effort is called for to reduce energy use. Much useful research is already in progress for breeding nonleguminous cereals capable of fixing their own nitrogen and hence to reduce nitrogenous fertilizer use. More work is required to replace chemical pesticides by biological control systems. It is urgent also to intensify genetic breeding to provide basic cereal crops with greater resistance to insect and fungal damage and also to various possible changes of climate.

In the field of transportation much interesting work is in progress and, in view of the desirability of encouraging communal travelling, new, flexible systems of urban transportation are urgently required.

Science and Technology for Development Disparities between developed and developing countries in Science and Technology are even greater than between their economic levels. Some 95% of the world's research and development is accomplished in the industrialized countries. It is true also that the poorer a country, the greater will be the proportion of its small number of scientists engaged in fundamental research. While the large developing countries such as Brazil, India and Mexico have an infrastructure able to support a significant extent of applied research and development, in the rest of the developing world there is little applied research, other than in agriculture. In such countries, merely increasing the number of scientists is unlikely to influence economic growth; indeed, it is more likely to increase the brain drain. This is because there is generally no employment for the scientists in the productive sectors. Science in these countries can only contribute significantly to development if it is intimately linked to the productive process.

It is generally accepted that a major—perhaps *the* major—need in the development of the South is the creation of an indigenous capacity in each country for research and development. This was the main conclusion of the UN Conference on Science and Technology for development held in Vienna in 1979, at which various financial and other mechanisms were devised to make this possible. After more than a decade there is little to show. Yet the need to build this capacity remains if the developing countries are to be able to enter the modern economy. There is a vicious circle here. If productive capacity is to grow and hence if development is to take place, a critical scientific and technological infrastructure is necessary, yet such an infrastructure seems impossible to build unless in symbiosis with the productive means. Finding means to overcome this impasse is a vital challenge to the countries concerned and to the international community.

3. The Role of Mass Media

The impact of mass media on public opinion and individuals no longer has to be demonstrated; a larger and larger part of humankind is henceforth deeply marked by the radio and television programmes it has access to, and there is something apparently obvious about discussing the power of the media in contemporary society. For better and for worse the media are one of the main agents in forming public opinion and the thinking of individuals.

The role of mass media, however, has so far never been deeply analysed in all of its dimensions. We know very little about the nature and duration of their influence. We are reasoning more on the basis of impressions and hypotheses than on clearly established facts; even in the West, the phenomenon is still recent and the reasoning is founded on the reactions of Western public opinion. In developing countries the phenomenon is even more recent and of still quite limited scope, which makes the study of the reactions of opinions in these countries more problematic.

The reactions that have been recorded so far are for the most part critical when they are not outright negative; the responsibility of journalists is frequently criticized, as are their subjectivity and their lack of respect for professional ethics. But the general role of mass media is too new for us to be able to draw definitive conclusions on it. This is why it is fitting to consider the question of the true power of mass media and that of what role they play and can play in the building of the new global society. The answer to these questions necessitates a dialogue with communication professionals in view of finding out what role they are ready to assume, not only for a better comprehension by the public of the world problematique but also in the challenge of the resolutique.

Experience shows that the power of the media so often referred to is not just an impression. There is no question about the reality of such power; consider, for example, the role of incitement played by transistor radios in the Algerian war of independence, or the pressure borne by the press in the Watergate affair, which led to the resignation of the president of the United States.

The media also represent a balancing power in democracies by exposing political or financial scandals and by defending consumer interests. It is true that they are always vulnerable to some degree of manipulation—whatever the political regime—due to political pressure, economic interests, disinformation procedures or even self-censorship. Mass media, especially television, have acquired considerable power over the last two decades; they have not however reached the maturity and responsibility which the exercise of such power would require. Where development is concerned, television has often complacently displayed atrocious images of the hunger and death of children in Ethiopia and Sudan, images that seem to have been taken out of Nazi concentration camps. Viewers across the world have been amply exposed to the sensational aspect of underdevelopment and have had their sensitivity brutally struck.

But doesn't the public expect, in fact, this dramatic version of information? A frightening event induces curiosity and the newspaper headline claiming "War tomorrow!" will sell more than one that states "Peace tomorrow." Part of the public likes images of war, death, underdevelopment and children dying of hunger. The need to entertain is dominant. But we do not intend here to study the public's deep motivations. We must keep in mind, however, that the media are business concerns and have to respond to public demand, whether they are public or private, that they work on the principle of making profits and investments and that they sell a very particular product: information, an overly abundant and varied—but perishable—commodity . . . in a context of severe competition to boot.

Can journalists therefore be said to have the freedom to write what they will? And that is not all. Depending on the governments and the times, underdevelopment is sometimes a subject to be disguised in countries that claim to be developing; in other cases, it is on the contrary a reality to be emphasized in order to support a request for financial or humanitarian aid. Environmental deterioration, the demographic explosion, local conflicts, hunger, malnutrition and poverty, the interdependence of nations are among the topics that can be treated from completely contradictory angles.

The selection of great world issues as well as of everyday news items gathered from among the five continents is an authentic problem: if the selection criterion is the latest news, the fact that the whole planet is its framework makes it so plentiful that it rises and falls in terms of its novelty and urgency and induces a feeling of scattering, dispersal and kaleidoscopic discontinuity.

We must insist, however, that the global approach to the world problematique is almost always absent. The catalogue of problems is reeled off on the air in no particular order without so much as an analysis of the causes or a suggestion of the solutions, however modest. It all depends on how much and what is considered to be newsworthy. This underscores the public's feeling that we live in a world of problems so enormous that any individual action would be in vain. The general reaction is one of stress, that is of a demobilization tending to turn people towards their personal problems and away from those of the world that surrounds them. The possible ways to solving the problems posed are not known about and the public feels overwhelmed, useless and parasitic.

Television daily faces a mass of information that has to be sorted out and selected on criteria that cannot possibly be completely objective and that vary according to the country and the leanings of the journalist. The task is all the more difficult as, by its very nature, television has to simplify issues that are in fact increasingly complex. A victim of the abundance of subjects and the news pushing it forward night and day, television rarely takes the time to get to the heart of a matter. What television newscasts cannot do must be taken over and explained by feature programmes, educational programmes and round-table discussions. Environmental and pollution issues are timidly making an appearance in feature programmes, while development is just beginning to be treated in its positive aspects.

We previously mentioned in our recommendations a number of more specific subjects that have to be brought to the attention of the public through educational programmes such as environmental protection, energy saving, the role of science and technology, the interdependence of countries in the North and those in the South and what this means for each of them, etc. The freedom of information, the free access of all to information and the pluralism of information remain the noble causes of battles never totally won and forever to be waged again. In the process of adapting to change, of continuous learning in a transitional society, of adjusting to uncertainty and complexity, the role of the media becomes considerable.

It will certainly be necessary to engage in a broad debate with the journalists and the top media executives involved to study the conditions for them to be able to define this new role. This is an initiative the Club of Rome will certainly take as the first step of a long dialogue.

X

MOTIVATIONS
AND VALUES

WE RETURN ONCE MORE TO ONE OF THE
main motifs of the contemporary scene, the dominant
influence of technology in the way it shapes our lives
and that of society. Starting from the Industrial
Revolution, we have gradually adapted our aspirations and life-styles to an ever more sophisticated and
pervasive technology which has permitted the enjoyment of what has been seen as material progress. This
has, of course increased the prosperity of a wide
range of citizens in the industrialized countries, reducing many of the grosser forms of poverty, improving health conditions, extending life expectancy,
providing general if not always appropriate education, and introducing many social amenities. Recognition that technology has a determinative role in
world development is relatively recent; even today,
the economic system which relies so heavily on technological solutions to problems has not yet fully
come to terms with it. It is still implicit in the think-

ing of many economists that technological development arises from the interaction of economic forces and is, as it were, one of the muscles of Adam Smith's invisible hand. There is no doubt much truth in this; however, more and more technological innovations derive from discoveries in the scientific laboratories and could not have been foreseen. Therefore science which has to be seen as an autonomous force gives rise to economy-motivated technology in creating new products and systems, and hence new demands.

Despite the unwanted social and ecological side effects of technology, and the general suspicion it has aroused because it spawned the nuclear bomb and genetic manipulations, generalized expectations of ever-increasing affluence flowing from it and of more and more material possessions persist within an economic system driven by the stimulation of consumer spending and credit availability. The luxuries of yesterday become the necessities of today; planned obsolescence speeds up the turnover of goods; the wastes of society accumulate and are even more difficult to dispose of as scientific sophistication diffuses into the everyday goods of the material bonanza.

There is, of course, another side to the coin. Considerable amounts of wealth from economic growth have been diverted into the creation of social goods—unemployment benefits, health services, education and welfare measures to reduce poverty. In a number of countries, this has been so strong as to evolve to become the welfare state which has psychological costs as well as social benefits. For instance, it is felt by many that the welfare state approach encourages an overreliance of individuals on the state, with an unhealthy lowering of individual responsibility and initiative. The paternalism of employers, so resented by the trade unions, has been replaced by state paternalism whose huge bureaucracies are, in turn, regarded as distant, faceless and impersonal.

The materialistic technology-based approach to development has penetrated into societies and cultures of all types, and even the most rigid, fundamentalist cultures find it impossible to resist the promise of power and affluence which it appears to offer. The goal of material affluence seems to generate greed and selfishness. Not that these features have ever been absent in individuals and societies, but they appear to have been magnified with the shrinking of nonmaterialist values as well as having become more apparent through disclosures of corruption, crime and financial scandals by the media.

The shortcoming of science is that although it has contributed greatly to our material well-being, promoting health, increasing the lifespan, giving us leisure, it has done little to enrich human existence, in comparison with directly material improvements. The imperative need now is to attempt to master and stimulate technology within a human framework, so as to contribute to the general and sustainable well-being of all peoples in this and succeeding generations, within a holistic, global and even cosmic comprehension and to balance material advances by cultivating social, moral and spiritual attributes. This is becoming true in the developing countries as it is already in the industrialized countries.

"Our present civilization is based materially on an extraordinarily successful technology and spiritually on practically nothing."

Dennis Gabor

The components of the corpus of society and, indeed of the individual's being are out of balance; the emotional, spiritual and even the intellectual elements have been overwhelmed by the weight of our physical triumphs. The establishment of a sane equilibrium can only come through a deeper understanding of the individual human being, a full awareness of our motivations which honestly accepts both their negative as well as their positive aspects and a creation within the self for the growth of wisdom and creativity. The problems, both of each individual and of society, lie deep within human nature; without an intensive knowledge of inner limitations and potentialities and overt recognition of these, our approach to problem-solving must remain at the level of recognizing symptoms of a disease undiagnosed. Attempts to prevent war, for instance, can never finally succeed until we understand the arising of conflict within each one of us.

Egoism, of which selfishness is a manifestation, or "the life force," as it used to be called in the first flush of Darwinism, is a property of all biological species and provides the primeval urge to survive, to reproduce, to prosper and to excel. It is the driving force of innovation and progress. But it also constantly manifests itself in selfishness, greedy and antisocial behaviour, brutality, lust for power (however petty), exploitation and dominance over others.

The struggle between the positive and the negative aspects of egoism is the eternal Faustian drama we all perform. The achievement of a dynamic equilibrium between its two opposing sides is the central but seldom-admitted objective of social policy. Too much latitude given to the exercise of the egoistic urge may produce a dynamic society, but it can lead to exploitation, absence of social justice, corruption and oppression.

We are haunted by our genetic inheritance. The negative aspects of our nature that we find difficult to admit even to ourselves—such as greed, vanity, anger, fear and hatred, which are manifestations of the brutality of our egoism—have served our species well through the long process of organic evolution, in achieving dominance over all other species of creation and over weaker races of *Homo sapiens* and pre-*Homo sapiens* which have long since disappeared. Now, having reached our present state of consciousness, aware of our own mortality and able to look into the future as the generational continuum of life, the negative features are of less use to us in the struggle upwards. But they persist and have to be taken into account in personal and collective behaviour. For centuries simple people have been disciplined and their negative features held in check to some extent by the hope of paradise and the fear of hell, but with the widespread loss of faith in religion and indeed in political ideologies and institutions, restraints have disappeared and respect for the law has decreased, giving rise to further terrorism and crime.

Our generation feels the absence of a sense of self, and it does not know where to look for it.

These features, projected from the individual to the collective level, operate correspondingly in the social environment. National egoism is likewise ambivalent; it can express itself as a natural and desirable love of country or ethnic community, or it can be whipped up to chauvinism, xenophobia, racism, hatred of other countries or styles of living and finally to war. In international negotiations it often surfaces as advocacy of narrow self-interest against the wider harmony and future well-being of a group of nations, including its own, and often seems to sacrifice longer-term self-interest to score immediate tactical points.

These matters are seldom admitted, and when they do emerge, they are shrouded in taboo. If this diagnosis is at all valid, there would seem to be a need for lifting the taboos and honestly acknowledging the existence and power of the negative and positive aspects of individual and collective behaviour, and for adopting an approach based on the enlightened and common self-interest of every inhabitant of this small planet to ensure that sustainable physical and social environments can be achieved for ourselves and our descendants.

This self-centredness, however, is merely one aspect of a broader question: what are the spiritual and ethical values, if any, that will constitute a foundation for the new global society, the emergence of which we are observing today?

A New Basis for Moral and Spiritual Values

"Oh stealer of songs, my heart!
Where will you find them?
You are needy and poor,
but grasp firmly the black and red ink wisdom,
And perhaps you will no longer be a beggar."

Aztec poetry,
MSS Cantares Mexicanos,
Fol 68, r.

The global society we are heading towards cannot emerge unless it drinks from the source of moral and spiritual values which stake out its dynamics. Beyond cultures, religions and philosophies, there is in human beings a thirst for freedom, aspirations to overcome one's limits, a quest for a beyond that seems ungraspable and is often unnamed. Experience has shown that no dictatorship, no violence, no restriction has ever managed to wipe completely out of man's heart this often invisible, often passionate quest constantly surging forth from the collective unconscious analyzed by Carl Jung.

At the same time, individuals and groups increasingly place this issue at the forefront of their preoccupations. Thus does the South Commission presided over by Julius Nyerere express in its last report[1] a very clear position in that respect, which shows evidence of an encouraging rise in awareness:

[1] 1990.

> In the final analysis, the South's plea for justice, equity and democracy in the global society cannot be dissociated from its pursuit of these goals within its own societies. Commitment to democratic values, respect for fundamental rights—particularly the right to dissent—fair treatment for minorities, concern for the poor and underprivileged, probity in public life, willingness to settle disputes without recourse to war—all these [. . .] increase the South's chances of securing a new world order.

Noble declarations such as this, which formerly inspired the behaviour of individuals and societies, no longer seem to be acceptable in contemporary activity. In the behaviour of people and of states, even those with constitutionally guaranteed rights, morals are flouted and the law ignored or twisted to suit the convenience of the authorities. In so many areas of relationships and communication, the implicit trend is "back to the jungle."

As already mentioned, humans have a need to possess a sense of self if they are to lead a life of decent human dignity. This was well understood in many traditional societies, but in the whirlwind of change it is very difficult to sustain. As a consequence of the many migrations, people are faced with cultural contradictions, often suffer a loss of identity, demoralization and have no meaningful work. In Western societies with their shallow consumerism, "I am what I own" or "I am what I do," the more fundamental aspects of life have shrunk, including those of religion, ethnic identity, inherited values and beliefs. Such a situation leads to hyperindividuality, selfishness of all types, overconsumption as well as an excessive search for distraction, for instance in TV viewing and drug addiction. There is a clear need for a new approach in which values are deliberately invoked to provide goals and a sense of meaning for the individual. However, change is too often seen as a threat to the self.

Have traditional values, then, been suddenly forgotten or abandoned? Have spiritual values been set aside all at once? What is the evidence? In our chapter on "The Human Malaise," we indicated that these values have in fact been progressively rejected by recent generations. In the industrial societies spiritual values have been eroded by the invasion of materialism which has also infected the elite classes in the developing countries. Again confusion on values arises in some countries from the crises in the major religions with their difficulty of adapting to the world in mutation without losing the essence of their message, as well as of responding to the serious questioning of the bewildered people of their congregations. Moral values are also becoming eroded, because they are flagrantly ignored by those who profess them, and by societies for which they are presumed to be the inspiration. Lax behaviour, selfishness and materialism appear to have made them irrelevant. But people are troubled by such symptoms. Never before has the issue of values been the object of so many symposiums, discussions and research. This demonstrates that beyond the shattering of the old value system, a need is being expressed with increasing intensity for a value system which would provide a basis of stability to the life of individuals and of society and which would give a basis of stability and the vision of a systematic world capable of leading to a systematic future.

Does this mean that a new value system is envisaged which would be in opposition to that of tradition? Or to the capacity of the traditional values to take a stand on the new challenges such as genetic engineering that ceaselessly trouble human conscience and judgment? Can we speak today of universal human values that would be common to all the inhabitants of the planet, beyond the diversity of their cultures?

The answers to these questions are not easy and yet they are what our future depends on: a global society can hardly be imagined without a base made of common or compatible values that will shape attitudes, the common determination to face up to challenges, the moral strength to respond and the management of change. We cannot want the emerging global society unless it is founded on the possibility of living together with the acceptance of differences and pluralism.

A large proportion of traditional ethical values are still valid today, though they may take different forms because of changes in the conditions of reference. Virtually everywhere, present-day society is more open, and richer, or at least aspires to a shared well-being. It is also better informed. For example, the idea of solidarity is changing from a concept limited to the family tribe to a much broader concept, while its strictly tribal connotation may be openly discredited.

To this end, pertinent ethical values may be defined and hopefully agreed upon if they are expressed in a way that is better adapted to the present situation. Among permanent values we would suggest freedom, human rights and responsibilities, family life, equal rights for men and women, compassion for the aged and the disabled, respect for others, tolerance, respect for life and peace, the search for truth.

> True words are not pleasant
> Pleasant words are not true
> A good man is not a speechifier
> A speechifier is not a good man
> Thus a good man is content with being resolved
> without resorting to force
> May he be resolved without pride
> May he be resolved without exaggeration
> May he be resolved without ostentation
> May he be resolved out of necessity
>
> Lao Tse

It is necessary to distinguish carefully between the individual and the collective level. In many cases they are compatible. The fight against pollution provides a good example. Indeed the interdependence of nations and the globalization of a number of problems calls for a raising of universal awareness and for a new international ethics. At the collective level we note a number of new approaches dictated by the pressure of the new facts:

- the ethics of nature, imposed by global environmental issues;

- the ethics of life,   exemplified by genetic engineering;

- the ethics of development,   resulting from the increasingly and unbearable gap between the rich and the poor;

- the ethics of money,   because it is divorced from economic realities and dominates the ambitions of too many individuals;

- the ethics of images,   which should rule over the media and modulate the influence of television in excessive dramatization of the image;

- the ethics of solidarity,   dictated by the fact that the dimension of the problems posed to humankind today requires co-operation between human beings as a condition of their survival.

A new ethical vision such as this will necessarily have repercussions on the national level.

In conclusion, the speed of evolution and of current mutations leads us to consider that the time factor has an ethical value in itself. Every minute lost, every decision delayed means more deaths from starvation and malnutrition, means the evolution to irreversibility of phenomena in the environment. No one will ever know for sure the human and financial cost of lost time . . .

Once this has been said, the ethics of solidarity and of time leads to an ethics of action, where each citizen must feel concerned and mobilized. The isolated individual always feels helpless in face of the immensity of the battle in the midst of which he is surprised to find himself. This induces individuals to organise and associate to find together the force and the effectiveness which they cannot muster when alone.

Collective ethics depend on the ethical behaviour of individuals and it is obvious that, inversely, the adhesion of the individual to a set of ethical behaviours can be encouraged, invited and aroused by the collective approach.

How can different traditional and modern, collective and individual value systems co-exist in a society and at the individual level?

The emergence of certain universal values such as human rights or respect for nature does not mean the end of ancestral values. They may contradict each other; in addition, individual values may at times conflict with collective values, or one value may conflict with another. A glaring example is the conflict between the sale of arms, which is a source of profit for a nation and of work for numerous men and women and yet is in opposition to the same nation's desire for peace.

The harmonious co-existence of very different values is nothing new, but it has been seriously questioned by the rise in fundamentalism. It is rather the relative importance attached to the values that changes according to the age of the ideology or religion in sway. Since each person is biologically and socioculturally unique, the emphasis should be laid on the individual aspect. "Collective" values are often the outcome of a choice made—or, worse yet, imposed—by those holding the reins of power, who want at all costs to impose their values by showing contempt for those of others, by even attempting to suppress them. "Collective" values can be taken into consideration only when there exists true freedom and a high level of culture.

Elites everywhere reconcile easily despite the surface controversy. The general public is not involved, only manipulated, in debates of this type. The gulf between elite thinking and thinking at a popular level is enormous. Here is where we find distortions and tensions difficult or even impossible to resolve.

An interesting and important point is that different value systems do in fact co-exist even though their co-existence is sometimes colored by opposition and mistrust. Indeed, it is not so much a question of the co-existence of contradictory value systems as of the same values being interpreted in different terms. When all is said and done, the factor that makes such co-existence possible, as well as the plurality of interpretations and the society of uncertainty, is the capacity for dialogue and communication.

To conclude this brief outlook, we must stress two phenomena that are going in opposite ways. There is indeed a weakening of the moral sense of individuals, who feel cheated not only because the ethical structure that used to serve as their reference and to which they willingly submitted has collapsed, but also because the great threats of the contemporary world have frightened them into a chilly self-withdrawal. Simultaneously, there is a progressive collective awareness of the great problems of the world, old and new, which is encouraging expectations and research. The spiritual and ethical dimension is no longer an object of scorn or indifference; it is perceived as a necessity that should lead to a new humanism.

"May the divine Spirit protect us all; may we work together with great energy; may our study be fruitful and thorough; may there be no hatred between us."

Aum, Peace, Peace, Peace, Peace
Vedic prayer (3000 B.C.)

LEARNING OUR WAY
INTO A NEW ERA

WE SHALL MAKE NO ATTEMPT TO SUM-
marise our conclusions; indeed the very nature of the
problematique precludes such a possibility. Instead
we shall make some observations and suggestions as
to how to blaze a trail into the thicket of the future
through learning, which is a leading feature of the
resolutique. Before doing so, however, we shall re-
state a few guiding principles that are scattered
throughout the book:

- the need for the involvement and participation of everyone in seeking a way through the intertwining complex
  of contemporary problems;

- recognition that the possibilities of positive change reside in the motivations and values that determine our
  behaviour;

- understanding that the behaviour of nations and societies reflects that of its individual citizens;

- acceptance of the postulate that dramatic solutions are unlikely to come from the leaders of governments, but that thousands of small, wise decisions, reflecting the new realization of millions of ordinary people, are necessary for securing the survival of society;

- effect given to the principle that privilege, whether individual or national, must always be complemented by a corresponding responsibility.

As stated in the introduction, the ideas and action proposals of this book are offered as a basis for learning our way into the future. It is not necessary—indeed it would be impossible to expect—for there to be complete agreement on all the thoughts we have expressed with regard to the world in revolution, or on the relative importance we have given to the various problems. The material presented here should rather be regarded as matters for widespread discussion and debate; it is intended to spark off a variety of examinations and reassessments on the part of those responsible for the management of society at all levels. Beyond this, it is hoped that the many whose contacts with governance are quite remote, but whose future is deeply involved in the changes to be foreseen, will begin to more clearly understand the significance of many of the topics presented such as the interdependence of the nations and the interaction of the problems. The time has come to show how every individual is more or less directly concerned with the problems of the world and the changes that are brewing, even if he or she can more easily perceive the symptoms than their causes. Even now, few remain untouched; one has only to mention the problems for some of co-existence with immigrants of different ethnic origins, the effect on children and adolescents of certain television programmes, the internationalization of automobiles or the international spread of the products for sale in supermarkets.

To learn our way through this period of transition and to identify sure points of reference, we have to modify our reasoning, our mental images, our behaviour and the realities on which we base our judgments so that we can understand this world mutation, with its array of global issues such as the environment, food security, development of the poor countries, the crises of governance and all the others we have attempted to describe.

The situation of complexity and uncertainty will condemn decision makers at all levels—and especially the politicians—to search for new approaches and to adopt untraditional attitudes. But it will not be possible to implement their decisions, no matter how brave and how pertinent, unless they succeed in obtaining wide public support. However, general resistance to change and fear of the unknown constitute an unfavourable environment to strong, but unfamiliar action. The dynamics of public opinion will not be able to operate usefully, unless the individuals who make it up have access to the nature of global phenomena and acquire, through their understanding of them, the conviction of what is at stake—the very survival of the human species. It is obvious, however, that the eloquence of the facts alone will be insufficient to convince individuals that these phenomena are of immediate concern to them. To most people they will seem distant, theoretical and too vast in comparison with the problems of everyday life, their family, professional, financial, health and day-to-day survival problems. The scope of these difficulties may well elicit a reaction of withdrawal, a refusal to understand or anxiety at the thought of the individual in his helplessness and isolation having to grapple with a set of facts that are mind-boggling in their variety and complexity.

Such doubts and alienation will have to be acknowledged and deliberately addressed so that they can be dispelled by shared fears and a familiarity with the facts gradually achieved through discussion with others. The situation must be seen in local and personal terms. This is one reason for the need for a revitalization of democracy on a more participative basis, stimulated by comprehension of the global concerns.

The need, then, is "to think globally and act locally." The Club of Rome has, from its beginning, realized the need for such an approach and there are a multitude of ways in which it is or could be achieved. We offer a few examples in the following.

GLOBAL–LOCAL INTERACTION

On the initiative of Maurice Strong[1] and the Club of Rome, a meeting was held in 1989 in Denver with some forty Colorado decision makers to discuss the following question: In what ways do the great world problems affect the economic and social life of the state of Colorado and in what way can the political and economic leaders of the state exercise an influence or have an impact on these great problems? Dur-

[1]Secretary General of the United Nations Conference on Environment and Development, member of the Club of Rome.

ing the work and discussions of the meeting, interaction became more and more evident in a number of areas and especially on environmental issues. If every inhabitant in Colorado makes energy-saving as well as fighting against waste his or her daily duty, the action will have repercussions on the situation of Colorado, therefore of the United States, therefore of the world. If the individual is alone, the result will be merely symbolic. If a number of individuals join to act in the direction of better environmental protection and if their influence in the community strengthens their fight, then the result will be significant. The Denver meeting was followed by an open forum in which the ideas and conclusions of the small, restricted meeting were shared with a large audience of the general public. Similar meetings are being planned in other countries, initially in Japan, and similar approaches are being taken by other bodies and sometimes even by governments.

In a different area, that of development, we underscored[2] the role of local initiatives in the development process, often taken by nongovernmental organisations, groups of villagers and the like with action on farming, health and hygiene, education, etc. Corresponding activities are also spreading in the big-city slums and both of these are contributing to modifying the concept and the global vision of development policies, for which they have provided the reality of experience in the field that is the reflection of the multiplicity of geographic, cultural and human situations.

The Club of Rome, in disseminating its concerns

[2]See Chapter 7, Development versus Underdevelopment.

and encouraging the emergence of global thinking in local action, has encouraged the creation of National Associations for the Club of Rome. These now exist in about thirty countries in the five continents. The Associations are governed by a common charter, some of the articles of which insist on the nature of the interaction of the local and the global:

> Each Association shall approach the global problems in terms of the country's own cultural values and thus contribute to the general understanding of the human condition on the planet.
>
> It shall have the duty to disseminate locally to decision makers, academics, industrial circles and the public at large, the reports, findings and attitudes of the Club. It shall contribute experience, creative ideas and proposals, towards the understanding of the global problems, to the Club.

The National Associations for the Club of Rome have, therefore, the mission of bridging communication between the national realities and the problematique as seen nationally on the one hand and the global thinking of the Club on the other, and acting as relays for the circulation and dissemination of Club thinking in each country. Going from global to local and from local to global is a radical transformation in modes of thinking and reasoning which will become essential henceforth. It is a new intellectual exercise which we shall have to extend and integrate.

LOCAL INDIVIDUAL INTERACTION

The picture would be incomplete were we not to address the action possibilities of the individual human being who is at the centre of the entire edifice. In extreme cases such as the threat of war or natural disasters, individuals are immediately transformed into citizens, aware of their responsibilities and ready for cohesive action. Other, less spectacular but likewise significant examples bear witness to the fact that individuals are not inert and indifferent in the face of imminent dangers. When there is an environmental threat close by, or when a situation arises where people's interests are at stake and gross instances of exploitation are revealed, we find that initiatives are taken in the most diverse fields by individuals and small groups prepared to fight for causes that affect them directly or indirectly and by which they feel motivated.

Suffice it to mention as examples transportation or telephone users' organisations, or in a different category, NGOs that care for disabled children, old people or battered wives; again there are NGOs in the fight against AIDS and a host of other diseases, NGOs in the struggle for human rights, ecological NGOs, peace groups and a multitude of developmental NGOs such as we have presented above. Neither must we forget the initiatives in many countries by the jobless to create employment for themselves or to set up their own businesses as well as the NGOs that were founded to assist small businesses and to provide them with technical assistance.

Individual commitment to action of these sorts is therefore possible and already widespread, which demonstrates that a link can be established between the human being and local or national actions, which, in some cases, flourish, extend and become international.

The Emergence of the Informal Sector   The success of grassroots NGO initiatives no longer needs to be demonstrated. Very often, these movements are sparked off by individual men and women. Examples throughout the world are multitudinous. In the Indian state of Uttar Pradesch, the local people have rallied around a man called Sunderlal Bahuguna to stop the construction of a U.S. $1.7 billion dam, which would have submerged their villages and seriously increased the danger of avalanches in the region. Several reports that questioned the technical feasibility of the project, added to an eleven-day fast by Bahuguna, led the government to back down on its plans. In Kenya a woman, Wangari Maathai— founder and President of the grass-roots Green Belt Movement and member of The Club of Rome—has led a successful battle to stop the construction of a sixty-two-floor office-building in a popular Nairobi public park. In Mexico City, where the problem of pollution has gone far beyond bearable limits, Marcos Chan Rodríguez mobilized his neighbourhood to form a grassroots group to reduce the operations of a cement factory that was pouring cement particles into the air. In the process, the group realized that to arouse the ruling party's interest, it had to appeal to the left-wing opposition, and therefore make the democratic system work.

The enormous proliferation of NGOs can be seen in every sector of national and international activity;

some are strictly professional, others represent special interests; they may be single-issue groups or deal with general concerns; they may have a religious orientation or be based on a particular political ideology. The arising of this wide variety of NGOs is a healthy phenomenon which demonstrates that the human fabric is able to react to the rigidity and to an apparent impotence of national and international official structures in face of current problems. This new pattern of informal bodies has little coherence and often appears somewhat anarchistic because it is marked more by spontaneity and flexibility than by its concern with structure—something it is wary of. Most of the innumerable new NGOs are weak, financially and otherwise, but their lack of power is often compensated by vigour and enthusiasm. In a few cases such as that of the "greens" they may even try to penetrate the official structures by presenting candidates for parliament. In other cases, for example that of the Worldwatch Institute of Washington, surveys of world trends are scrutinized seriously by political personalities in many countries.

This new, so-called informal sector is beginning to be taken seriously by governments and international institutions, often with some reluctance and despite the apparent incompatibility of what is official with that which is not. However, some NGOs possess experience, insights and knowledge that governments lack, as well as representing significant elements of public concern which cannot be ignored. Thus some co-operation is emerging between the official and the informal and this is proving useful to the latter as different NGOs meet and discover their similarities and differences. We feel that similar co-operation is necessary also in the international fora. Intergovernmental discussions tend to be even more sterile and distanced from reality than those on the national level and hence a leavening of the debate by inclusion of a few carefully selected nonofficial experts in the committee could be inspiring. We have already suggested this in putting forward the idea of a UN Environment Security Council.

Despite more and more frequent meetings where several NGOs come together, their objectives and effectiveness remain scattered and generally unknown for many NGOs. Without meaning to advocate the structuring of the informal sector which might easily lose its soul in the process, a more effective system of mutual information would avoid much useless dispersion, encourage a fruitful exchange of experience and lead to the creation of alliances, thus increasing overall effectiveness.

This is one of the areas which the Club of Rome will pursue in its new initiatives. Although global efforts are essential to face some of the inescapably global issues, we must continue to operate at many levels—global, regional, national, provincial and local. At times we need not jump too quickly to the highest level, when local or regional efforts can be more successful. In fact, substantial impacts can be made, even on the largest-scale issues, through multiple actions on a small scale.

INNOVATION IN LANGUAGE, ANALYSIS AND APPROACH

In so many of the elements of this global revolution, we lack knowledge and indeed there is no guarantee that more research will lead to greater certainty or that research will yield its results in time for them to influence decisions which are urgently required now.

We know a lot, but we understand very little.

We have therefore to learn to act in face of continuing uncertainty. Politics has always been the art of making decisions under conditions of uncertainty. The difference today is that the uncertainty is much deeper and is compounded with rapid change. This abiding uncertainty demands adaptation of our institutions and approaches to achieve greater flexibility and a greater capacity for reaction as we keep our sights on the moving targets of history.

A central challenge in this connection is how to reconcile the economic language and concepts that dominate today with environmental language and concepts. Two approaches are possible: environmental aspects can be added to conventional economic analysis, or economic approaches can be integrated within a broader ecological view. Great care and precise thinking are needed in this area, in which distinction must be made between different types of economics: macroeconomics, microeconomics and environmental or ecological economics. We must find ways of integrating environmental aspects more effectively with the established and powerful approaches of both macro- and microeconomics.

The role of the market and its relation to that of government is of vital importance in seeking to resolve and manage the environmental problems. No solutions based exclusively on the market exist in the real world. All Western countries, for example, have developed mixed economies in which governments provide a framework of regulations, incentives, support and guidelines to the private sector. It has been acknowledged that the market approach alone cannot handle problems of common property resources or issues of long-term common interest. Government must provide the boundary conditions in the public interest.

The problems we face are not only intellectual and analytical; real interests and the structure of power are always at stake. In the real world, contradictory interests are inevitably operating. In establishing a normative approach, arrangements on action have to be established between power groups and, indeed, between nations which will evidently continue to have different interests, values, norms and cultural traditions.

The Values on Which Action Is Based

We must be more explicit about the importance of values and ethics in the different areas of the problematique, for this will become a battleground for the future and a fundamental ingredient for the resolutique. If we accept concern for the prospects of future generations, we cannot escape consideration of how the problems and values of the present generation will influence these prospects. Our efforts to create a sustainable world society and economy demands that we diminish the profligate life-styles in the industrialized countries through a slow-down in consumption—which may, in any case be forced on us by environmental constraints. The ethical imperative also implies renewed efforts to eliminate poverty throughout the world.

The ethical approach has not thus far been a matter of major concern, to say the least, for decision makers in politics and business. At the very most we can find a cloudy ethical reaction among the public at large in their stands against corruption, against pollution and against a conception of the economy which appears to forget that it should be above all designed to serve men and women.

In the Western countries there exist, as we have said, frameworks of legislation to regulate the operations of the market forces, antitrust and antidumping laws, fair trading agreements credit controls and the like as well as codes of good practice often implicitly accepted by the business community. Such measures are necessary to ensure smooth and acceptable running of the capitalist society, to prevent fraud, to protect the work force and the public. While there is a degree of ethical motivation in the regulatory system, many of the measures are matters of convenience to provide propitious conditions for economic progress. Ecological disasters, sometimes causing death and destruction, raise these matters to a new level of importance and force industry to accept a degree of social responsibility in its own long-term self-interest, despite the fact that the costs involved threaten next year's bottom line. More and more it will be necessary to develop the recognizable ethical norms that society demands and with which industry can live, albeit uncomfortably. These should be matters of current concern for the Eastern European countries now accepting the system of the market forces with somewhat uncritical enthusiasm.

An ethical conception of international relations, which the world badly needs, cannot evolve unless it is also the inspiration on the national level and finally on the individual level as well. The development of